GREAT-GRANDMAMA'S WEEKLY

THE GIRL'S OWN PAPER

This magazine will aim at being to the girls a Counsellor, Playmate, Guardian, Instructor, Companion and Friend. It will help to train them in moral and domestic virtues, preparing them for the responsibilities of womanhood and for a heavenly home.

from the Editor's Prospectus, *1880*

THE GIRL'S OWN PAPER

TO THE EDITOR

OF

THE thanks of grateful girls to you
H erewith are sent (they are but due);
E ach girl has found a friend most true.

GIRLS had no Paper of their own;
I 've wondered why the *Boys* alone
R ejoiced in theirs, like folks up-grown,
L eaving the Girls to sigh and moan,
S aying, " To *us* no favour's shown."

OWN we the pleasure now 'twill be
W hen, as each week comes round, we see
N ew tales in prose and poetry.

PAPER for Girls! most happy thought!
A nd one that must with good be fraught.
P lease let us thank you as we ought;
E nvy is past—we're now, in short,
R ich in the treasure you have brought.

GREAT-GRANDMAMA'S WEEKLY

A Celebration of The Girl's Own Paper 1880-1901

Wendy Forrester

LUTTERWORTH PRESS
Guildford and London

First published in Great Britain 1980

ISBN 0 7188 2450 4

Filmset in Bembo 270, 11 on 12½ pt, quotations 10 on 11 pt, captions 10 on 11 pt italics and index 9 on 10 pt.
Printed offset litho in Great Britain by
Butler & Tanner Ltd, Frome and London

To
my Grandmothers
FLORENCE WILLIAMS
and
MARY FORRESTER

The author would like to thank Ann Hugh-Jones for a considerable amount of help and advice in writing this book.

CONTENTS

"ALL SOLD, MISS. WOULD YOU LIKE TO ORDER THE
JANUARY PART IN GOOD TIME?"

Editorial Note

Although the full and correct title of the magazine was *The Girl's Own Paper*, it was frequently and affectionately referred to without the definite article, or merely by its initials, and both usages have been adopted for this book.

G.O.P. stands for *Girl's Own Paper*, and *B.O.P.* for its brother publication, the *Boy's Own Paper*.

Material in square brackets has been added by the author.

All quotations are from the *Girl's Own Paper* unless otherwise stated.

Illustrations

The illustrations used in this book were photographed from original issues of the magazine and are reproduced by courtesy of Lutterworth Press and the United Society for Christian Literature, descendants of the Religious Tract Society.

The title page illustration is an acrostic taken from the issue of February 21, 1880.

VOL. I.—No. 1.]   JANUARY 3, 1880.   [PRICE ONE PENNY.

Amiable ever, but weak-minded never,
Brave in your duty be rather than clever.
Choice in your friendships, then true to your friend,
Doing nothing to vex her, much less offend.
Elastic in spirit, soar high as the kite,
Finding strength in the guidance that limits your flight.
Gentle in manner and gracious in speech,
Honey distilling the youngest to reach.
Idle young fingers make old slattern hands,
Just pinning, where method good sewing commands.
Kill crossness with kindness and make it relent,
Led captive by kisses and taught to repent.
Make merry at home for mirth is a treasure
Not meant to be wasted in frivolous pleasure.
Obedient and truthful, twin sisters of love,
Priceless as pearls from God's casket above.
Quarrels! Oh, let not such evil be wrought,
Religion forbids it, yea, even in thought!
Seek (earnest in prayer) for grace to restrain
Tempers unholy which give others pain.
Useful abroad, be more useful at home,
Virtue for service need never far roam.
Woman is formed from girlhood's first plan—
Xanthippe or Claudia, Queen Mary or Anne.
Young friends to be happy, now learn to be wise,
Zeal without knowledge is a head without eyes!

The Girls' Own Alphabet
from the first issue
January 3, 1880

THE PRINCESS VICTORIA.

FOREWORD

When I was a child, my father brought me, as a surprise present, a giant volume, the 1890–1891 *Girl's Own Annual*. During the years which followed, this gave me a good deal of pleasure, and I appreciated it even more when I was older.

In spite of my affection for this book, it did not occur to me until long after I was grown up that Annuals for other years probably existed; but when I did realise this I started to hunt, and before long acquired my second *Girl's Own Annual*, dated some years earlier than the first. I found the second equally delightful, looked for and discovered a third, and was well on the way to a collection.

A stack of stout books grew, some in plain dark bindings, some elegantly embossed with gold designs, all with dates in the eighteen-eighties and 'nineties. Later ones I rejected—though I might not be so strong-minded now—partly because I found the twentieth-century G.O.P. slightly less appealing than the Victorian one, partly for the simple reason that the volumes take up a lot of space and one has to stop somewhere.

I continued to spend many a peaceful hour reading the improving serial stories, the budgets for girls of slender means, the fashion notes, the answers to correspondents, and the other enjoyable contents of my growing collection, and one day it occurred to me that I had the material for a short feature comparing this Victorian magazine with one for present-day teenagers. I started the feature, but could not get beyond the first few hundred words, and eventually came to the conclusion that what I really wanted to write was a book about the G.O.P., during its Victorian years.

I believe that there may be people interested in reading a little about this popular and successful magazine for girls in the last century, and in that belief I have provided, not a history of the *Girl's Own Paper* in its Victorian years, but a dip into its pages which I hope may amuse, or inform, or perhaps both.

Although the chapters which follow review the magazine only up to the end of Queen Victoria's reign, it survived into that of her great-great-granddaughter. In its seventy-six years it underwent several changes of

Far left: this portrait of Queen Victoria as a girl appeared as frontispiece to the first issue of The Girl's Own Paper *(January 3, 1880), which included a description of her early life. "If Victoria has been a good queen, as well as a good wife, a good mother, and a good woman, this is due, under God, to the training she had in childhood and girlhood."*

GREYFRIARS.

A STORY FOR GIRLS.

By EVELYN EVERETT GREEN.

"TRIX CAME RUNNING IN."

CHAPTER XVI.

JESSIE'S FIRST APPEARANCE.

WHEN Esther's footstep had died away along the corridor, and Jessie had locked her door upon the intruder, a different look came into her face; all the would-be indifference and weariness vanished in an instant, to be replaced by a vivid excitement and triumph, which gave a wonderful brilliance to her beauty, whilst robbing it of something of its youthfulness and childlike quality.

"You can come back, Thérèse," she said, softly, "I think we are safe now. At any rate the door is locked."

At these words there appeared from an inner dressing-closet, the door of which had been carefully closed, the French maid, who bore in her hands a pile of rich white drapery, and several cases which evidently contained jewels. Upon her sharp dark face was a look of cunning which was not pleasant to see there, and in her voluble fashion, half French, half English, she began discoursing on Jessie's beauty, on the ravishing appearance mademoiselle was about to make, on the delight and astonishment of the Vicomte at the sight of his princess thus attired, and the blissful conclusion which must come as a *finale* to such a charming little romance.

And whilst she thus talked, in a fashion that would have disgusted Esther, and which no mother, even an indulgent and not overwise one, would have tolerated for a moment, Jessie sat

---

Above: an episode from the serial Greyfriars, *by Evelyn Everett Green, from* The Girl's Own Annual, *1890–1891. Abetted by a sly French maid, Jessie decks herself for a forbidden ball, to her tomboy sister's admiration. "Oh, Jessie, you are a stunner!"*

name and format, finally disappearing under the title of *Heiress*, in 1956. The Editor's farewell letter expressed the hope that it would reappear in easier times. However, the nineteen-sixties, waiting in the wings, was not a decade in which a magazine like the *Girl's Own Paper* would have been likely to flourish, retitled or not. A 1949 copy saved from my schooldays seems nearer in spirit to the *G.O.P.* of the eighteen-nineties than to one of the teenage magazines of fifteen years ago. It would have been even less likely to survive in the nineteen-sixties than in the comparatively congenial atmosphere of the years just after the Second World War. However, it may be welcomed back by another generation. I hope it will.

INTRODUCTION

The first issue of *The Girl's Own Paper* appeared on January 3, 1880, published by the Religious Tract Society in Paternoster Row, London, price one penny.

Just a year earlier, with the express purpose of counteracting—"nay, of destroying and throwing out of the field"—the spate of "pernicious" publications arising in the wake of the 1870 Education Act, the Society had launched the *Boy's Own Paper*. The lively and progressive style of this magazine was an experiment, a departure from the Society's established religious periodicals (*Sunday At Home*, *Leisure Hour*, the *Child's Paper*), and considerable misgivings were voiced among the more conservative dignitaries of the Committee, dedicated as they were to the moral and spiritual welfare of the nation's youth. But—"I think every reader ... will find that however exciting or interesting it may be, it is pervaded by a Christian tone," the Earl of Aberdeen, a former chairman of the Society, assured them. The immediate success of the venture came as a revelation, as did the fact that the paper's readers numbered girls as well as boys—eighteen-year-old Georgina Hamilton, for instance, winning a prize for a competition in an early issue. Very soon it was clear that there was wide scope for a feminine equivalent of the *Boy's Own Paper*.

However, although the *Girl's Own Paper* closely resembled its brother in appearance, it was by no means a *B.O.P.* with the sexes changed. The adventure stories so much associated with the boys' paper are rare in the Victorian years of the girls'—the greatest adventures for them being those of love and marriage, or of earning one's own living. Nor are there many school stories of the kind so popular with a later generation, where the heroine has ten to make and the match to win, and where chums converse in elaborate slang. The tone of the paper is less "schoolgirlish" than "girlish", and possibly the Editor might have preferred it to be described as "womanly".

Fiction was the mainstay of the magazine, with two serial stories running at any one time, and occasional short stories. There were articles on health and beauty, dress, needlework, housekeeping, cookery, hobbies, music (actual scores were printed from time to time, and Queen Victoria's youngest daughter, Princess Beatrice, was a contributor), foreign countries, doing good, poems, jokes and anecdotes (termed *Varieties*), competitions and a weekly collection of answers to correspondents. Appropriately enough, the first issue was graced by a girlhood portrait of the Queen, thus setting the tone.

"There was a real want of a paper which girls could truly call *their own*," recalled the Editor years later in the thousandth number (February, 1899), going on to say:

A paper which would be to the whole sisterhood a sensible, interesting and good-humoured companion, counsellor and friend, advocating their best interests, taking part in everything affecting them, giving them the best advice, conveying to them the best information, supplying them with the most readable fiction, and trying to exercise over them a refining and elevating influence ... Success shone upon us from the very first, and *The Girl's Own Paper* at once and by general consent took a foremost place amongst the magazines of the day.

Professional critics in the press were generous, and said many a friendly word in our praise. The late George Augustus Sala [a popular journalist] elevated *The Girl's Own Paper* to the position of "first favourite", and in an encouraging notice expressed a hope that "all the girls" of Great Britain would subscribe, for he thought it would be greatly to their advantage. Much-valued approval and friendly letters of advice and help also came to us in these early days from Mr John Ruskin, who, writing to a girl friend, said that he had ordered the paper to be sent to him regularly, and added, "Surely you young ladies—girls, I ought to say—will think you have a fair sixpennyworth." [Monthly numbers containing the four weekly issues bound together in blue covers were priced sixpence.]

Evidently the girls agreed with Mr Ruskin. The magazine proved extremely popular, its circulation quickly rising to over 250,000 and eventually outstripping even that of the boys'*; and the timely revenue from both publications enabled the Religious Tract Society to increase its support of its many mission stations in Africa, China and Catholic Europe. At the end of the magazine's first year, the Society's annual report noted that "some of the Society's friends have complained of the [B.O.P. and G.O.P.] as being too secular in tone", but added that "the attempt to give them an exclusively religious character would be to defeat the very purpose for which they were intended". Fortunately this purpose was not defeated and by the fifth month the gratified Committee had recorded their sentiments:

There was an urgent need for such a publication.... We earnestly and with thankfulness believe that the hopes expressed in our preliminary prospectus ... are being fulfilled—that *The Girl's Own Paper* is to its readers a guardian, instructor, companion, and friend, and that it is preparing them for the responsibilities of womanhood and for a heavenly home.**

The review attempted in this book of the magazine's first twenty-one years will, it is hoped, enable today's readers to judge whether at least the earthly hopes of the publishers were fulfilled.

Far right: on October 5, 1895, the G.O.P. published a setting by Princess Beatrice of a song by Queen Victoria's dear Disraeli, which recalled with "smiles and sighs" the long-lost days of youth.

---

* Patrick Dunae, *Boy's Own Paper: Origins and Editorial Policies*, The Private Library (journal of the Private Libraries Association), Second Series, Vol. 9, No. 4, Winter 1976.

** Rev. S. G. Green, *The Story of the Religious Tract Society*, R.T.S., 1899.

H.R.H. THE COMPOSER

THE GREEN CAVALIER'S SONG.

Words by The EARL OF BEACONSFIELD.   *Music by* H.R.H. PRINCESS HENRY OF BATTENBERG.

I re-mem-ber, I re-mem-ber when life was like a May-day flower; I re-mem-ber, I re-

THE EDITOR

Throughout its Victorian existence, and for some years later, the G.O.P. had only one Editor, Charles Peters, who came to the R.T.S. from Cassells.

In the thousandth number, in 1899, he wrote: "To the Editor-in-Chief of the Society's magazines, Dr Macaulay, the hearty thanks of the Editor are due for liberty of action and a great deal of kindly encouragement." A deleted entry in the Minutes of July 20, 1882, however, suggests that he had earlier been criticised for over-secularisation: "A hope was expressed by the Committee that Mr Peters would act more in harmony with the principles of the Society."

Clearly there is the mark of a very strong editorial personality on the magazine. His successor, Flora Klickmann, called him "an editor of strong individuality" in the appreciation which opened the 1908–1909 Annual, at the end of his tenure:

The death of Charles Peters, who had been the editor of this magazine for twenty-eight years, came as a personal loss to tens of thousands of readers who never saw him. There are piles of letters in my office at the present moment from people who never met him, nor ever exchanged a letter with him, all regretting his death as though he had been an intimate friend. And the reason for this is clear to all those who have followed, month by month, year by year, the pages of this paper. From the very first, Mr Peters had but one aim in editing this magazine, viz. to foster and develop that which was highest and noblest in the girlhood and womanhood of England, helping his readers to cherish their finest ideals, and teaching them to see the things of life in their proper perspective, putting the best things first, and banishing the worthless from his pages.

It was inevitable that before long he became something far more than an ordinary editor to his huge constituency. Not only the girls for whom the magazine was originally started, but their mothers also, made him their final court of appeal when in any doubt or difficulty, and in this way he became the personal friend and counsellor of multitudes who would not have known him had they met him face to face.

And no man took his work more seriously, striving to the last to give the magazine his very best. It was no wonder that when he passed away he left a blank that no one can really fill and hosts of friends to mourn his loss.

THE MAGAZINE

By the time these words appeared, the *Girl's Own Paper* had become very clearly an Edwardian publication. The new editor chose to re-title it *The Girl's Own Paper and Woman's Magazine*. The weekly numbers, price one penny, were discontinued, and a more compact monthly issue replaced them, selling at sixpence, as the old monthly had done. Flora Klickmann gave her reasons for the change (1908):

In the days when *The Girl's Own Paper* was started, girls had not so much pocket-money as they have at present, but now any girl can afford sixpence a month for her magazine, and would rather scorn to take it in pennyworths ... [Moreover] when the magazine started it was intended for girls only, but very soon it became apparent that it was being read by grown-ups as well ... the girls of the past have become the grown-ups of today, and are still taking in the magazine.

Far right: the Editor's Christmas greeting to his readers, December, 1881. (The same design was thriftily used again many years later.)

16

I PRAY THAT GOD MAY BLESS THIS CHRISTMAS DAY
OUR FRIENDS AND KINDRED ALL

J. M. Kronheim & Co.

With the kind regards of the Editor of The Girls' own Paper.

OUR NOVEL CHRISTMAS-TREE.

My wife will be delighted. See, my dear,
Here's one *you* little thought could be so
   near."
(*Hostess advances, and Host, turning again
to Father Christmas*)—
"We hardly hoped to see your face again
So soon, but trust you will remain
And share our pleasures."

    FATHER CHRISTMAS (*shaking hands with
Hostess, and addressing her*)—
        "Shall I not intrude?
In coming thus will *you* not deem me rude?"
    HOSTESS—
"My husband's friends are mine, but I, as well,
Have known *you* longer than I care to tell.
Where are the children? Kiss me, little
   Snow."
     (*Kisses her, and turns to Frost*)
"Shake hands, my boy. Dear, dear, how
   they do grow!"
(*Fog, who has been hanging back, here
steals into the room and hides, as well as he
can, behind one of the unlighted trees, as if
afraid of being seen by Father Christmas,
who is now seated. The Hostess, assisted by
servant, hands refreshments to Father Christmas, Frost, and Snow, but does not observe
Fog in his hiding-place.*)

CHAPTER III.
THE TREE!

A LOUD knock is heard at the door. Host
rises to open it, and holds up his hands in
great astonishment at seeing Father Christmas, who enters, followed by Frost, Snow,
and a servant carrying, *apparently*, heavy
carpet-bag and parcels which are put down
near the trees.
    HOST (*shaking hands with Father Christ-
mas*)—
"My very oldest friend! I do declare!
A thousand welcomes! take this easy chair.

    HOSTESS (*addressing Father Christmas*)—
"I am *so* grieved that such an honoured guest
Was not in time to sup with all the rest."
    FATHER CHRISTMAS—
"Don't name it, pray, I only can be blamed,
And, at so late an hour, I feel ashamed
To trespass on your kindness by a call."
    HOSTESS—
"A hearty welcome meets you from us all;
We're only too delighted you have come,
And that you find us, with our friends, 'At
   Home.'"

Throughout the eighteen-eighties and 'nineties, however, the changes were slight. Issues looked very like each other, printed in three columns of rather small type. Illustrations were line drawings, except for the rare "presentation" colour plates. In addition to fashion drawings and fiction illustrations there were occasional full-page pictures, with such titles as *Maiden Meditation*, *Sweet Seventeen*, *Fair Daffodils* and *The Flower Girl*, tending to have something of a family resemblance.

The first page of each number was headed by the upper half of a female figure with flowing hair, an expression of extreme spirituality, and no pupils to her eyes, bearing the title of the magazine on a banner. TWO LITTLE GIRLS wrote in 1880 about this figure, apparently worried about the blankness of the eyes, and were told:

The figure at the head of our paper is not the copy of a picture or portrait, but of a statue. It is not the custom in art to put eyes on statues of pure white marble. In the later and lower periods of Greek sculpture, statues were sometimes coloured, but no one now expects white marble to have eyes like dolls or wax figures. The statue of which our heading is a copy has been greatly admired. It was called by the sculptor "The Spirit of Truth and Love", and we think this a good motto for our paper. Our engraving was made from a photograph expressly sent for *The Girl's Own Paper*, by Mr S. C. Hall, Editor of the Art Journal. . . .

In 1893 the Editor decided that this heading had been used for long enough, and held a competition for a new one, open to all, professional and amateur, men and women. It would be pleasant to relate that a girl reader was successful, but the design chosen was by Henry Ryland of Kensington. The new heading appeared in October 1894 and depicted two young women in classical draperies, one drawing, one writing. Viewed rationally, it is more pleasing than its predecessor, but perhaps things are not quite the same without the soulful lady.

Other changes began to be noticeable about the same time. Photographs appeared, somewhat fuzzy, and instead of the delicate, detailed line illustrations there were halftone ones, still monochrome—more dashing, but rather less attractive. Early in the new century there was a major change in the appearance of the magazine, with larger print and two

Above: Henry Ryland's prize-winning design for the new masthead which showed "two maidens artistically attired in white sitting in graceful ease"

Far left: Our Novel Christmas Tree, Ruth Lamb's account of preparations for a Christmas party, complete with the text of the special charade written for the occasion by Mamma, appeared in January, 1880.

Far right: captioned Biding Their Time, *this illustration appeared in the issue of April 16, 1892.*

columns instead of three. The extra Summer and Christmas numbers were romantically titled—*Silver Sails, Sheets o' Daisies, Lily Leaves, Victoria's Laurel, Rosebud Garden, Mignonette*—*Christmas Roses, Snowdrops, Feathery Flakes, Household Harmony, Christmas Cherries.*

THE CONTRIBUTORS

"The Editor has been assisted in his labours by a band of very willing workers—authors, musical composers, and artists—whose names are familiar to all our readers," Charles Peters wrote in the thousandth issue. To mark the anniversary, a hundred of the contributors presented him with an autographed tea-table cloth, recognising "the ability, friendliness, and discretion which have been all along displayed in his dealings with his staff". He was ready to cast his net widely, and wrote of himself:

Whilst surrounded by a tried staff, he has made it a rule to welcome contributors—indeed, to invite them—from every quarter. . . . Amongst our occasional contributors may be seen the names of a queen, several princesses, and leading members of the nobility, and a great many more who have distinguished themselves in various lines of activity connected with the life and work of women and girls.

Lists of the year's contributors were published at the front of each Annual. To take, at random, the volume for 1888–1889, the list of seventy writers includes one Queen (of Roumania), one Countess, one Baronne, four other titled ladies, one Baronet and five Reverends★. Also present as a young man of twenty-three is the poet W. B. Yeats. Among some fifty artists listed, three are Royal Academicians, including James Sant, "Principal Painter In Ordinary to Her Majesty".

A gallery of photographs of the regular contributors was published in the 1884 Summer issue, *Sunlight*; when this idea was revived in the thousandth issue, some fifteen years later, many of the earlier faces were still there. The Editor in Chief, James Macaulay, depicted in 1884 with flowing beard and skull-cap, looked conservative and stately in 1899; Charles Peters appeared modestly in the midst, a rather solid, round-faced man.

One of the chief regular contributors was Gordon Stables, M.D., C.M., R.N.; veiled under the pseudonym "Medicus", he was the author of the regular articles on health and beauty. This seems an unlikely profession for a Naval doctor, but he must have found it satisfactory since, like the Editor himself, he was connected with the magazine for nearly thirty years, writing in addition to his health and beauty articles other features, under his own name, on a wide variety of subjects—notably on animals. (At the same time he was contributing similar articles to the *Boy's Own Paper*, and writing adventure stories.) Reference to the Medical Register of 1880 reveals him as a graduate of the University of Aberdeen (he remarks on his "kilted knees" in an article about a Scottish holiday), with

★ Contributors included the Rev. W. J. Foxell, B.MUS., a member of the Religious Tract Society Committee. The Society is now the United Society for Christian Literature, proprietors of Lutterworth Press, who are the publishers of the present book, and whose General Manager is Mr M. E. Foxell, the contributor's grandson.

BIDING THEIR TIME.

THE HOLIDAY:
HOW TO MAKE THE BEST
OF IT.
By MEDICUS.

DIFFIDENCE isn't a virtue, and it certainly isn't a vice; it is something that we rather like to see in a young girl, and can just pity and forgive in a boy; and yet—would you believe it?—it is the feeling uppermost in my mind at the present moment. And if you will listen to me I will endeavour to explain to you how it happened to come there. I looked into our Editor's room a little while ago. It was early in the day, but he was busy, as usual; he was flanked on both sides by piles of letters and flowers, and a load of manuscript lay before him, so that I could only get a kind of bird's-eye view of him.

"How do you do?" I said. "I hope I see you in good health."

"Are there two *p*'s in apartment?" was the Editor's reply, not deigning to lift his head, but scribbling away as if writing for his life.

"No," I said, "only one *p*. Good morning; I must be off."

"Wait a moment," said our Editor. "I want you."

Now the fact is, I didn't want to be wanted. I had my dust clothes on. I presume I looked quite gay. I was bound for a long drive. However, there was nothing for it but to wait, so I sat down on a pile of old papers, and hung my white hat on a file. After the lapse of five long minutes he looked up.

"What are you going to give us for this month, Medicus mine?" he said. "You must write your article *now*."

"This is beautiful weather," I replied, "and everybody is out."

"Duty first," said our Editor; "duty first, doctor. Now what is it going to be? The eyes of two hundred thousand young girls are on you; and *there* is paper and *here* is a pen."

"What would you say," I said, "to an article on the circulation of the blood?"

"Circulation of the blood, indeed!" said our Editor, scornfully. "Who do you think would read it? Our girls can feel their blood circulating, they don't need to be told of it.

No, tell us something practical. Be useful if you can't be lively."

I cast only one longing, lingering glance at my white hat on the file, took up my pen and commenced, merely remarking to the Editor, "I don't mind losing a holiday for the sake of our girls."

So now, my fair young readers, having sacrificed my own holiday for your sakes, I trust you will let me give you some hints which, if taken and adopted, will assuredly tend to make your holiday all the more agreeable to you.

And here is where the diffidence comes in. Your boxes are all packed, your flyman is at the gate—he has come fifteen minutes before his time, as flymen often do—and you are all bustle and excitement, and I, your Medicus, touch you gently on the shoulder. No wonder I am diffident for daring to address you at such a supreme moment. Well, then, don't read my article just yet: fold THE GIRL'S OWN PAPER carefully up, and slip it in under the rug-

his address given as the Naval Medical Service—this no doubt owing to his nomadic life; he spent much of his time touring the country in a caravan called "The Wanderer", with his dogs—a St Bernard and a New-foundland are mentioned. His photograph in the magazine reveals him wearing very long moustaches, and looking younger than the avuncular, "no nonsense" style of his articles would lead one to imagine, though he was already forty when he started writing for the G.O.P. in 1880.

Although the *Girl's Own Paper* was edited by a man, the feminine touch was by no means lacking. Most of the fiction and many of the features were written by women. One of the chief fiction authors was Ruth Lamb, already an established novelist when the magazine was launched. Her first by-line in the G.O.P. was for *Our Novel Christmas Tree* in the second issue in 1880, a charming account of the pleasantest kind of Victorian family life. Over the years she contributed a number of serial stories (*Her Own Choice, Only a Girl-Wife, One Little Vein of Dross*), among the most interesting those with a socially reforming message (*Sackcloth and Ashes*). In 1896, by then calling herself "an old lady" and signing her letters "your affectionate mother-friend", she was contributing a regular religious or "thoughtful" feature, *In the Twilight Side by Side*, and running the Twilight Circle, to which girls could write with spiritual problems:

LIDDLE, C. (British Guiana).—Your letter, dear girl, has made me very glad. Every day brings new proof of the delightful bond of union which our Talks in the Twilight have established between girls of many nationalities. . . . [1901]

IRIS (Simla).—I have not heard from NORA lately, but if this meets her eye, I am sure she must feel deeply the interest taken in her, and the many prayers offered for her by you and members of our Circle all over the world . . . Your words are sweet and cheering, dear IRIS, and of late I have joyfully acknowledged so many hopeful messages from my girls. . . . [1901]

The names of Dora Hope and Dora de Blaquière recur frequently over a number of years—two of the contributors who seem most thoroughly journalists, both displaying a practical versatility over the whole period. Dora de Blaquière wrote, for instance, *Winter Clothes and How to Make Them, St Valentine's Day, Books Before Travel, Grilling and Devilling, On Helping in the House, What Should We Afford for Dress?* Dora Hope's most characteristic productions were articles on domestic economy cloaked as fiction (*She Couldn't Boil a Potato, The Brothers' Benefactor*) but she turned her hand to a variety of subjects—in the first volume alone, *How to Make Poor Children's Clothing, How to Embroider in Crewels, Pressed Grasses and Ferns for Ornamental Purposes, How I Managed my Picnic, A Girls' Walking Tour* and *Sunday School Work*.

Although the very first serial story, *Zara*, was anonymous (there was more anonymity in the earlier issues), the second, *More Than Coronets*, appeared under the name of Mrs G. Linnaeus Banks, who must have been a valued acquisition, already known for her popular novel *The Manchester Man*. First published in 1876, it had gone through four editions within as many years.

Rosa Nouchette Carey was another extremely popular and prolific novelist. Her earliest book, *Nellie's Memories*, had sold thousands and was followed by many successful stories. She wrote a number of serials for

GORDON STABLES, M.D.

DORA DE BLAQUIÈRE.

Far left: an article by Medicus published on July 30, 1881. A delicate girl going on holiday must take proper flannel underclothes, stout shoes for evening (to avoid catching cold through the feet), sensible stockings and a shawl or plaid. She must rise early, get plenty of exercise, drink as much milk as she can, and be sure to pack a good tonic.

IN CHURCH.

By W. B. YEATS.

SHE prays for father, mother dear,
  To Him with thunder shod,
She prays for every falling tear
  In the holy church of God.

For all good men now fallen ill,
  For merry men that weep,
For holiest teachers of His will,
  And common men that sleep.

The sunlight flickering on the pews,
  The sunlight in the air,
The flies that dance in threes, in twos,
  They seem to join her prayer—

Her prayer for father, mother dear.
  To Him with thunder shod,
A prayer for every falling tear
  In the holy church of God.

Above and far right: published on June 8, 1889, companion to an article called What Shall We Do With Our Sundays?, *was this poem by the young W. B. Yeats, with its gently idealised illustration.*

the G.O.P. (*Merle's Crusade*, *Esther*, *Little Miss Muffet*), while Macmillan and Co., who published many of her books (Blue Cloth, Gilt, 3s. 6d. each), quoted *The Lady* magazine describing her novels as "immaculately pure, and very high in tone", and the *Pall Mall Gazette* as doubting "whether anything has been written of late years so fresh, so pretty, so thoroughly natural and bright". In 1899 she was living in Putney with her widowed sister and another very long-standing G.O.P. contributor, the poet Helen Marion Burnside, who compiled the Rosa Nouchette Carey Birthday Book, with introductory verses, in 1901.

Lily Watson contributed besides serial stories (*A Fortunate Exile*, *The Hill of Angels*), articles such as *Self Control* ("The young lady who in any crisis instantly becomes useless by dropping into insensibility, or both useless and actively objectionable by 'going off' into shrieking hysterics, is no longer regarded as fulfilling her vocation"). Francesca Maria Steele (*The Convents of Great Britain*) wrote novels under the pseudonym "Darley Dale", and Elizabeth Emily Charlton chose the romantic name "Eglanton Thorne". Sarah Sharp Hamer (writer of children's stories as "Olive Patch") was the cookery expert "Phillis Browne" and wrote *The Girl's Own Cookery Book*. Among other important contributors were Isabella Fyvie Mayo, Sophia F. A. Caulfeild, Emma Brewer, Sarah Doudney, Nanette and James Mason. Anne Beale wrote serial stories such as *Restitution; or, Miser and Spendthrift* and articles such as *Our Tractarian*

IN CHURCH.

HER OWN CHOICE.

By RUTH LAMB.

" ' COMMON, DO YOU CALL HER ? ' CRIED A SHRILL VOICE, CLOSE BY."

Above: an episode from Her Own Choice, *a serial by Ruth Lamb (June 28, 1884). The heroine Hilda is deeply remorseful when her careless words are overheard by the mother of an injured child whom her tender-hearted cousin, Dorothy, has rescued.*

Movement. When she died aged eighty-four, she bequeathed her diary, in twenty-six volumes, to her friend the Editor, who published some extracts under the title *Anne Beale, Governess and Writer* in 1900. The popular *Pixie O'Shaughnessy* and *Peggy Saville* novels of Mrs de Horne Vaizey began to appear in serial form towards the end of the period, under the name "Jessie Mansergh".

24

THE READERS

"Anyone, with half an eye, can see that 'The G.O.P.' is intended for girls of all classes," wrote the Editor in 1880 in reply to a correspondent signing herself GREY HAIRS. He went on:

Girls of a superior position—belonging, we mean, to the "upper ten thousand"—should read everything, and be well up in *every* matter upon which we give instruction. Their money, time, and superior intelligence admit of this. For girls of a less high position there are papers on economical cookery, plain needlework, home education, and health. Servant-maids communicate to us well-written letters, and by their tone we can see that our magazine has indeed helped them to an intelligent carrying out of their humble work; that it has been a companion to them in their isolation and a counsellor in times of sore temptation. There is much in our paper we humbly believe that will train these girls in living a pure and honest life, and we rejoice to help them, for their letters convince us that there is honesty and nobility even in the kitchen. From our daily letters from the girls, written upon coronetted notepaper by those of noble birth, and by others from the kitchens of humble houses, we gather that there is help needed by all, and that our paper has given a high aim to their lives and a practical and wise assistance in their various engagements.

The Editor might have added that, as well as all classes, all ages and nationalities were also catered for. Between GREY HAIRS and six-year-old TOTTY CROOKES, who enquired about removing grease spots from silk ("We think Totty writes very well for her age"), there was something for everyone. The fashion features were written for grown-up "girls", as were the health and beauty articles; few of the serial stories had heroines younger than the late teens. Early competitions were sometimes restricted to girls under nineteen, but the interest shown by older readers resulted in later competitions having entrants in their thirties. Needlework competitions attracted industrious children as young as six or seven.

The popularity of the magazine overseas, particularly in the Colonies and Dominions, but also in America and Europe, is well in evidence in

A VERY young heroine, Miss Esther Mary Cornish-Bowden, aged eight years, has just been awarded by the Royal Humane Society its medal and a handsome testimonial explanatory of the circumstances under which she bravely entitled herself to receive that medal. She is the daughter of a gentleman living at Black Hall, Avonwick, Ivybridge, Devonshire, and she saved the life of her governess, Miss Bradshaw, who, when returning from Sunday-school on the 30th of November last, with the youthful heroine and her younger sister, turned giddy, and fell into a pond six feet deep with water. Dispatching her younger sister to the keeper's lodge, Miss Cornish-Bowden bent over the pool, trying to lay hold of her drowning governess. This she did, but in the effort, she overbalanced herself, fell into the pond, and sank. Never losing her presence of mind, she retained her grip of the governess, and when she rose to the surface she still held her by the right hand, while with the left she caught hold of some short bushes. In this position they remained for about five minutes, the child calling for help. Eventually a passing workman heard the cries, and assisted Miss Bradshaw and the child out of the water. The former was partially insensible, but her brave little rescuer appeared quite unconcerned.

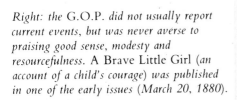

Right: the G.O.P. did not usually report current events, but was never averse to praising good sense, modesty and resourcefulness. A Brave Little Girl (an account of a child's courage) was published in one of the early issues (March 20, 1880).

Above: some answers to readers' queries, published on November 5, 1887. In the same issue the Editor advised LOLLY POP *and* E.B. *who wanted to be hospital nurses; referred separate enquirers to the Association for the Oral Instruction of the Deaf and Dumb, the Oxford Local Examinations Board, the Froebel Society; suggested that girls thrown out of work by the closing of a Sherborne silk factory might be sent to a training school for servants; and warned hopeful* CLARIE *that she would probably fail to make a livelihood out of embroidery.*

the correspondence columns; by the late eighteen-nineties there was a regular column devoted to International Correspondence.

Taking the whole circulation of *The Girl's Own Paper* from the issue of the first number [wrote the author of an article, *Looking Back*, in the thousandth issue] we arrive at an imposing result....

Suppose that instead of distributing the copies to subscribers, they had been hoarded up and made to form a tall pillar, one copy being laid flat on the top of another. And supposing a girl wished to read the topmost number—the present number, that is to say—without using a ladder, she would have to wait till she grew to be a hundred and seventy miles high.... If all the numbers which have been circulated since Number One were laid end to end, they would make a pathway long enough to go round the world at the Equator with a bit over.

Chapter One

THE
MODERN WOMAN

Too often ladies hide the fact that they have to work for their living, as if it were an everlasting disgrace and could never be forgotten. This is one of the old-fashioned ideas, which, it is to be hoped, a more enlightened age will wipe out. Only this week an elderly spinster, who has lived in highly-genteel poverty for the best part of her life, remarked to me, "My grandmother was a perfect lady— she *never did anything*." May future years be preserved from such nonentities!

How to Secure a Situation
(1892)

My friends call me an old-fashioned girl, some of them say eccentric. I know they mean commonplace, but that troubles me not; what does trouble me are the ways and doings of my up-to-date friends, those who pride themselves upon being anything but commonplace.

I will show you what I mean.

Perhaps it is because I grew up in an out-of-date place where the air blew fresh and sweet straight from the heavens, where everything around us was true and genuine, because my sweet mother and I were the closest of friends and companions, she teaching me to reverence my own sex as well as to respect the other, that I can no more revolt against her ideas and desires than I could rebel against the God who made me.

Because also in this quiet seed-time of my life I acquired what has been well-called the habit of "thinking-back," I have been able to keep myself together and avoid being carried along with the stream, since like many another country girl I have entered the busiest throng of busy bread-winners. It is not of the bread-winning girls that I am going to speak, however, so much as of those who belong to the leisured class, yet as one imitates another so much, the defects of the latter will often be found in an exaggerated degree among the former.

My occupation has given me a back-seat view of much in life which I could not otherwise have obtained a glimpse of; and a back seat is of all seats the most enjoyable if one can so far forget one's own existence as to be thoroughly interested in other people. From my quiet corner I have been able to watch the girls of our period, to judge them critically, to admire them immensely, and to be profoundly ashamed of them at times.

For anyone above the poverty line, a good case could be made for choosing the late Victorian period as a pleasant time to live. It was an era of comparative peace and prosperity, and among its principal advantages must be counted a sense of progress, reform, improvement. The franchise was being extended, primary education becoming universal, sanitation and medical knowledge improving, trade unions being given the protection of the law. Not every citizen can have welcomed every reform, but it is difficult not to assume a feeling in the air that life was changing for the better—particularly for women.

A girl who bought the first issue of the *Girl's Own Paper* when she was seventeen would not have been able to vote in a Parliamentary election until she was fifty-five (1918), but she was living in a world where women were gaining a place in education, business, and the professions, and where women's suffrage was at least being discussed as a possibility.

The majority of the magazine's middle-class schoolgirl readers would have attended private schools (seminaries for the "Daughters of Gentlemen"), though some would still be receiving their education at home from governess or tutor. Secondary education was left practically untouched by the State until 1902, though the Girls Public Day School Trust was setting up schools—later to be called High Schools—to prepare girls for further study at universities or other institutions of higher learning.

After school, a middle-class girl who stayed at home would probably be given a dress allowance by her father. A sum of £10 or less would

Above: the opening of an article, The Girls of Today, *by Lucy H. Yates (August 18, 1894).*

normally mean making her own clothes—"On a dress allowance even of £20 per annum I think there is little or no room for dressmakers' bills" (1883). Some girls might receive £5 a year with the responsibility of buying only their own boots and gloves.

Among the well-to-do, of course, were some girls who were given very substantial allowances, even as much as £100, but these would have been a very small minority. The usual age of "coming out" for a girl in society was eighteen, and although only those readers in the upper reaches could expect to be presented at Court, articles on the subject appeared from time to time and dealt in detail with every aspect of the ordeal, from walking backwards when wearing a four-yard train, to the number of plumes worn in the hair.

When a girl "put up her hair", it was a sign that she was growing up, and readers wrote to ask at what age this would be proper. "Girls usually put up their hair at about sixteen," the Editor replied to ESMERELDA in 1883. A few weeks later, NAPOLI was told, "Your hair should be turned at eighteen. It would look like a silly attempt to make a child of you for you to wear it down your back later than that." But many of the poorer girls, of course, wore their hair up in a bun, or tucked away under a cap, much sooner than that. They often left their Voluntary or Board schools before entering their teens (not until 1918 was it illegal to leave before the age of fourteen) to earn their own living; and for them the price of their weekly Girl's Own Paper represented no small sum. Nanette Mason, in the grim little feature How Working Girls Live in London, wrote:

The average weekly earning of girls engaged in labour of all kinds cannot be more, it has been estimated, than ten shillings.... No wonder that many of them look as if they never had a luxury in their lives. [1888]

But for the girl seeking to improve herself and her lot, the Girl's Own Paper must have been reckoned a good pennyworth. It is worth noticing that, in the budget for a ten-shillings-a-week girl suggested in the above-mentioned article, two pence is allocated "if she belongs, as we will hope" to a trade union. The feature, which ran through a number of issues, ended with the statement:

Were wages raised many good results would follow.... We are confident that a better day than was ever seen before has, in our time, dawned, though it may not yet shine brightly on our sisters, the working girls of this country.

By far the greater number of poor girls went into domestic service, and the G.O.P. encouraged this, feeling that young women were safer employed in private homes than in factories or shops. A thirteen-year-old maidservant might start her career at £5 a year, rising later to £12 or perhaps £18. The factory girl's wages averaged £21 to £34 per annum; the shopgirl's slightly more. An article entitled Bar Maids and Waitresses in Restaurants, Their Work and Temptations in an 1896 issue gave the average wage of these workers as from 5s. to 10s. a week (£13 to £26 a year), "subject to a charge of from 7d. to 9d. per week for breakages"; hours worked were often twelve to fourteen—and sometimes up to seventeen—a day. An assistant teacher in an elementary school might receive £50 a year, while a Post Office clerk or a trained book-keeper could earn between £65 and £80.

Far right: the opening of a short anonymous feature, A Contrast, from June 12, 1880. This drives home a favourite G.O.P. lesson. The heedless girls who deliberately order their ball dresses at the shortest possible notice care nothing for the overworked girls at the dressmaker's, among them poor Mary, who collapses from exhaustion, and dies in her sleep.

28

THE Misses Saunders were entertaining a select party of four of their intimate friends at afternoon tea. It was a cold bleak day in December, and without the wind was raging and howling, and fiercely driving before it the flakes of thick-falling snow.

It was the sort of day that makes you gather round the warm fire and feel thankful for the shelter of home.

The force of contrast made the cosy sitting-room where the girls were assembled all the more cheerful and inviting. It was a tastefully furnished apartment, abounding in the dead greens and black furniture so fashionable at present, and bountifully supplied with low easy chairs, which the girls had grouped round the hearth, where a glorious fire was blazing, lighting up the room, which was growing dark in the early December twilight.

Miss Saunders—familiarly called Gracie—presided at the little gipsy table, with its silver urn and tea equipage, while Lucia, her younger sister, handed cake and cups of tea to their guests.

They were all pretty stylish girls, but Gracie and Lucia were strikingly handsome, and both dressed in the extreme of fashion—"got up regardless of expense" as the others declared.

"I am sure it will be an extremely pleasant evening," Lucia was saying, going on with the subject which had been occupying the little party for the last half hour.

"Sure to be," assented the dark-eyed girl she addressed. "The Brownlows always do manage that sort of thing well. What are you going to wear, Gracie?"

Gracie turned round from her duties of teamaker with a merry laugh. "Don't you wish you may know, Carrie?" she answered; "but I'm not going to tell you. Last time we were at the Brownlows, Clarice got to know that I was going to wear pink, and then the dear good-natured creature wore red herself, and would insist on keeping close to my side all the evening, in an apparently affectionate way, but in reality because she wanted her red dress to kill my pink one. Then another time when I had ordered the dresses for Lucia and myself, what did Charlotte French do but steal the idea, and then appear at the same place in a dress exactly like ours, just for all the world as if a dozen had been made to order. I'm not going to give either of them a chance again; so Lucia and I have held a solemn conclave and have decided what we will wear, but we are not even going to give the order to Madam Robertson until two days before, by which time, I should hope, both Clarice and Charlotte will have made their own arrangements."

"That's not at all a bad idea," replied the girl who had spoken before. "It's awfully annoying to find one's ideas appropriated by some one else. But won't it be rather a hurry for you to get the things in time?"

"Oh no," answered Gracie carelessly. "Madam Robertson is very good, and always manages to let us have what we want by the time we name, and she never makes a misfit."

"But, Gracie," ventured, in a very gentle voice, a fair-haired girl, sitting on the hearthrug, holding a screen of peacock's feathers to shield her face from the fire. "Do you think it is *quite* considerate—I don't mean so much for Madam herself, as for the workgirls she employs? Mamma tells me that the poor things are sometimes almost worked to death because people give such short notices, and she always makes me give as long a one as I can conveniently."

CHRISTMAS EVE IN HAMILTON WARD.

Above: The Wards of St Margaret's, *by Sister Joan, a serial from 1894, follows the heroine, Constance, through thirty years of nursing, to end her career in spinster contentment sharing a cottage with her friend Hope.*

Requests from readers for advice on their careers were frequent, and the replies always well informed:

KATHLEEN.—Twenty-five is the earliest age to be admitted to several of the most important London hospitals, but in some institutions girls are accepted as probationers at twenty-one. Paid probationers usually receive £10 or £12 salary the first year, with board, lodging and uniform; but many girls nowadays are glad to pay £13 13s. for their training as the competition among would-be nurses is severe. [1896]

CATHERINE L.—Uniform of a hospital nurse is provided. Of underclothing, supply yourself with as much as you can afford, when of sufficient age to be eligible, which you are not till past twenty-one, even in a children's hospital. The usual age is twenty-five—very young people are liable to catch disease. [1896]

30

"WHAT SHALL I WRITE?"

The stage as a career was emphatically discouraged by the *G.O.P.*, which frequently warned readers against the awful dangers awaiting girls in the theatre:

Once on the stage, those wishing to leave it and live religious lives find much prejudice from prospective employers. [1884]

Too often an "educated" girl faced with the need to support herself thought no further than a post as companion or governess. A reader signing herself DESPONDENT wrote in 1896:

My father has died, and our comfortable home must be broken up. I am told that I may have £30 a year, but this is not enough to live upon. Could I become a companion?

She received the Editor's reply:

Above: The Marriage Settlement, *from the title page of the issue for September 1, 1894.*

31

Situations as companion are much harder to find than girls seem to imagine. They depend largely on private influence. Ladies take as companions girls of whose qualities they already know something. We cannot blame them for this. If there are any friends of your family who might avail themselves of your services, by all means make your wish known to them. But failing this, we earnestly recommend you to spend some portion of your money in learning a business; what this business should be we cannot suggest until we know your tastes and abilities. But think over matters, and then please give us some idea of your preferences, when we will with pleasure advise you more fully.

Governessing was a career which, although on the decline, still attracted a good many girls—though not all qualified, as a reply to one poor aspirant showed:

You seem to think that we keep a registry office. You are not sufficiently educated to take a place as nursery governess. You cannot write; and do not express yourself properly. [1894]

An article in 1884 dealt with *The Duties of a Governess*:

From the time the governess enters a house it should be her grand aim to win her pupils' love.... Continual fault-finding is too trying to a child's patience.

But the governess's patience, too, had long been sorely tried—and for such young women every year brought new options on to the horizon. In 1888 came *The Type-Writer and Type-Writing*:

Just now the type-writer is attracting considerable attention; and though its use in England is far from being so general as in the United States, we feel quite safe in prophesying that even in our comparatively conservative land, for many purposes the pen will be in a few years superseded by this ingenious machine. ... Type-writing is doing much, and will do more, towards solving the problem of finding suitable employment for ladies, it being an occupation peculiarly fitted for their nimble fingers. In the United States, lady type-writists are a large and important body, commanding good salaries, and as the instrument comes into general use in this country, ladies who have learnt to work it will have no difficulty in finding remunerative employment, especially if, in addition, they can write short-hand.

The *Girl's Own Shorthand Class* series of articles began in 1892:

The only requisites are Pitman's sixpenny "Phonographic Teacher", which can be got through any bookseller, a fine-pointed pen or pencil—not too hard to run easily over the paper, or too soft to make a delicate yet firm stroke—some ruled paper (say an old copybook), and a little patience.

Young Women as Journalists appeared in 1891:

Supposing the young woman to be mistress of all necessary accomplishments, she will still have to decide whether it would be quite seemly for an unprotected girl to travel about London or a great town in the evening until after midnight. The work also has to be done in all kinds of weather. We have seen such a girl at her work, and one who was apparently well fitted for what she was about; but we sympathised with her in regard to the hardships of her lot while we could not but admire her courage. As things are at present, the girl reporter has to assume a bold mien when, with her notebook, she takes her place at a table among perhaps a dozen men, on whose province she is encroaching. It is not an occupation which tends to the development of feminine graces; and this will be as fully realised by the girl herself as by those with whom she comes in contact....

Far right: The Tennis Players, *written by Sydney Grey and illustrated by Everard Hopkins, October 13, 1883.*

THE TENNIS PLAYERS.

By SYDNEY GREY.

Swift to follow the bounding ball,
  Active and lithe of frame,
Hark, how their voices rise and fall
  While merrily goes the game.
Laughter borne on the summer air
  Says life's true wealth is youth and health,
And a heart with never a care.

Yonder the grey-haired gardener moves
  Tranquilly to and fro,
Looks at the joyous group, and loves
  To think of the long ago;

Far-off years, when he had his share
  In life's true wealth, bright youth and health,
And a heart with never a care.

So grim age ever spoils our prime;
  Winter must follow May;
Each is best in its own good time,
  And wise in its ordered way;
But to the young is earth most fair,
  For life's true wealth is youth and health,
And a heart with never a care.

"HARK, HOW THEIR VOICES RISE AND FALL
WHILE MERRILY GOES THE GAME."

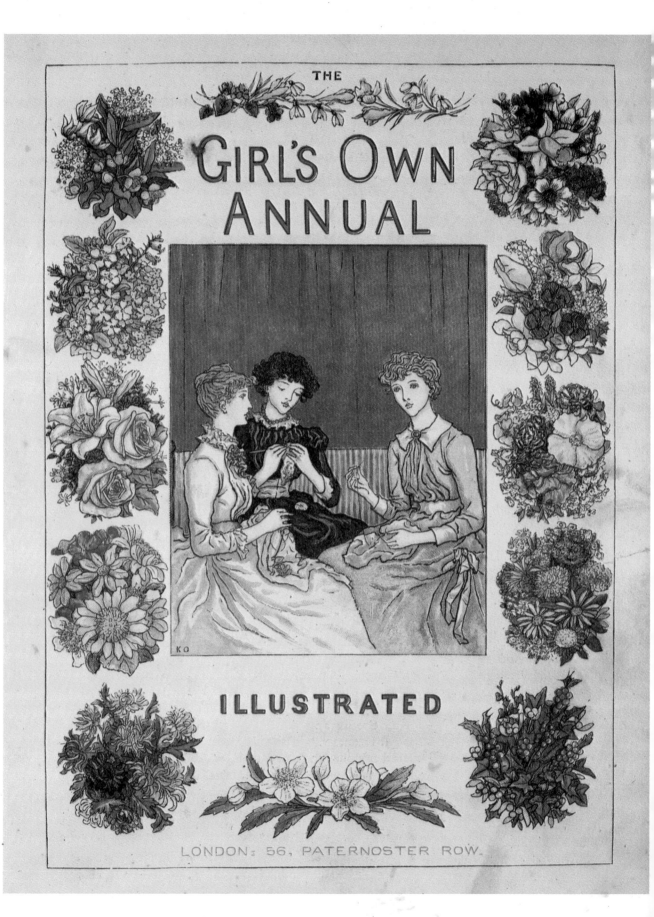

THE

GIRL'S OWN
ANNUAL

ILLUSTRATED

LONDON: 56, PATERNOSTER ROW.

But an aspiring and talented young woman need not turn her back on journalism because she does not choose to compete with ordinary reporters.... Reporting is only one branch of the profession.... Many accomplished journalists have never been reporters.... A great deal of the most effective work on our newspapers has been done by women; and, could it be told, the public would today be surprised to learn how much of the total is still done by them.

In *A Chat With a Girl Photographer* in January, 1901, the subject of the interview was a Miss Edmonds who had started as a "receptionist and shopwoman" with a Kensington photographer, and worked her way up until she had her own studio. Still a young woman, she attributed the success of her business to her up-to-date ideas:

The monstrosities which make up the usual photographers' "accessories" are conspicuous by their absence.... Balconies and pedestals, and pictorial backgrounds, with impossible perspectives, find no place here.

Some interesting figures on women in work were given in reply to a correspondent in 1894:

A BREAD EARNER.—We can give you statistics respecting the number of self-supporting women for the year 1892. There are 288,919 in the United Kingdom who are following various professions; 26,344 engaged in commercial business; and in our various industries and manufactures 2,027,899 more. These are all unconnected with those engaged in domestic duties. In Germany half a million more women are thus earning their living than those in our own country; and in Austria, France and Italy fewer earn their living than is the case here. Altogether, the number of women thus employed exceeds that of men by four and a half millions.

If prospects of advancement for the working girl were poor, those for women aiming for professional careers were brightening. In the field of higher education, major advances had been made. In 1884 the *G.O.P.* published *Education for Women at Oxford*, dealing with the question of admitting women to the University examinations, which was one so vigorously argued that a special train was chartered to bring from London all those who would vote in favour of the ladies. The article ended:

Some twenty years hence, when it has become a commonplace event for women to enter for these examinations, we shall look back with interest and amusement on the great struggle and the triumphant victory of the champions for the Higher Education of Women.

Despite this victory, Sophia F. A. Caulfeild had need to write tartly in 1894:

The justice and magnanimity which would show "honour to whom honour is due" ... is not always found equal to the occasion when it involves the granting of a degree.... St Andrew's, and the London Universities, and those of Chicago, Pennsylvania, Brown and Tufts, and Yale, stand by themselves in their fair-dealing with women scholars, admitting them to all their privileges and honours.... Only the other day the Royal Geographical Society refused the admission of women as Fellows, when at least Isabella Bird (Mrs Bishop) and Mrs French Sheldon might certainly have been regarded as well qualified for such an honorary distinction, and both ladies very worthy successors of the wonderful Ida Pfeiffer.

(Ida Pfeiffer [1797–1858] had been the subject of an article, *A World-Wide Traveller*, in an 1885 issue.)

Far left: the title page of The Girl's Own Annual, *1886–1887, drawn by Kate Greenaway. A reproduction of her drawing* Afternoon Tea, *with its characteristic blend of freshness and formality, was one of the presentation colour plates in the same volume. When she died in 1901, the G.O.P. published an appreciation.*

THE GIRL'S OWN PAPER.

"WOMAN'S RIGHTS."

By HELEN MARION BURNSIDE.

Oh, those boasted "rights of women,"—
    Rights, of which so much is said!
Yet what are they?—Can you tell me,
    Wedded wife, or learned maid?
'Tis a vexed and vexing question,
    Which I fain would understand,
Often asked, but never answered,
    Oh, my sisters in the land!

In the days lang syne, I'm thinking,
    Hearts were just as brave and true;
Woman's work was never wanting
    For a woman's hand to do.
'Twas our privilege and duty
    To shed light on Earth's dark ways,
Though we never talked, or dreamed of
    "Woman's rights" in those old days!

Ah! lang syne, lang syne, my sisters,
    There were women standing by
When the Saviour's feet went toiling
    Up the steeps of Calvary.
Women soothed the pain and anguish
    Of those hours, so dread and dim;
Theirs the right, so sweet, yet awful,
    E'en to minister to Him!

Such sweet rights are ours for ever,
    Oh, my sisters in the land!
Rights of ministry and mercy,
    To be wrought with heart and hand.
Think you that those "rights" you talk of—
    Make them whatsoe'er you please—
Can be deemed more honour-worthy,
    Or more high and dear than these?

Above: a poem by Helen Marion Burnside, whose verses frequently appeared in the magazine (January 7, 1893).

Far right: an illustration to verses by William Luff:

"Am I a lily growing?
Standing still in the light?
Drinking ever the dews of Heaven
All through the darkest night?"

(October 4, 1890)

Not all contributors, however, were so enthusiastic on the subject. In *The Vocations of Men and Women* (1890), the Reverend Dr Tremlett complained:

There are some who wish ... to convert this gentle, yielding, believing mind into the hard, unyielding, reluctant mind of a man. And when they have done it, what then? Have they raised the nature of woman? Nay, have they not rather lowered and perverted it? Depend upon it, man cannot alter what God has designed, and surely it is both unreasonable and unchristian to attempt it.

The gentle, yielding reader was advised in *Thoughts on the Higher Education of Women* by A Man in 1891:

The subjects to be avoided, save in an elementary manner, are mathematics, and possibly science—certainly, however, the former. The subjects most to be encouraged are classics and history. These two widen and refine, while the tendency of mathematics for women is to make them narrow, and creatures of only one idea.... Depend upon it, ladies, the judgment of the Cambridge undergraduate represents fairly the judgment of English manhood upon your sex; and if there is anything he hates and ridicules, it is a masculine, unwomanly woman.... He wants to find sympathy in his pursuits—true womanly sympathy; a helpmate, not a lady who understands differential and integral calculus, who will discourse learnedly and drearily upon one everlasting subject.

Despite objections such as these, the attitude of the magazine was in general encouraging—although early articles inclined to the traditionally "ladylike". *On Earning One's Living—Fruitful Fields for Honest Labour* in 1880 suggested sculpture in wood, engraving on wood, designing patterns, china-painting, book-binding, painting on panels, mosaic work, flower-making, frame-making and gilding, repoussé brass-work, sewing and millinery, kindergarten teaching, teaching deaf-mutes, dispensing medicine, reporting and short-hand writing, law copying, nursing, painting in water-colours, and oil painting. But in 1883 appeared a series entitled *Work for All*, in the first article of which the anonymous author wrote:

THE DISADVANTAGES OF HIGHER EDUCATION.

WE hear a great deal nowadays about the advantages of the higher education of women. During the last few years high schools have multiplied in every direction: colleges and halls have been opened at both Universities, and girl graduates are no longer *rare aves*.

Does not that mean that while the talented women of this generation are studying to equal men on their own ground they are leaving the women's posts for the incapables? If this comes to be the rule may God help the men!

Another side of woman's influence follows naturally on this. Do we not all know dozens, if not hundreds, of cases, even among our own friends, where "the unbelieving husband is sanctified by the wife"? Where the man who has been careless and irreligious is gradually brought into the right way by his wife? Where a mother's quiet wisdom keeps her sons straight, among the innumerable temptations which beset them, at school, at college, and on their going into life? Do we not all know at least a few of the women of whom it might be said—

"She never found fault with you; never implied
Your wrong by her right; and yet men by her side
Grew nobler; girls purer, as through the whole town
The children were gladder that pulled at her gown."

We cannot help thinking that the great fault of the education of the present day is that the learning is made an end, and not a means. There is an old-fashioned notion that education is a preparation for the work of life, and that no amount of knowledge can take the place of practical usefulness. No doubt a certain amount of knowledge is necessary to fit us for this life; but, married or unmarried, a woman (if only she knows what she knows, and is taught when a child to do her work thoroughly) can find plenty of work lying ready to her hand, and she will be far more useful doing than studying.

A woman's natural quickness of perception may often be of the greatest possible use in matters which seem above her ken; but if she tries to advance too far she will certainly fail. Dwarfs on giants' shoulders see farther than giants; but we all know the fate of the dwarf who fought by the giant's side.

M. P. S.

THE STAMP SNAKE (*page* 332).

Now comes a question—Is this altogether advisable? Are there not great disadvantages as well as advantages connected with this system?

It is well known that a woman's *physique* is not equal to a man's, and the brain power depends very much on the *physique* which nourishes the brain—*ergo*, the average woman will never equal the average man on his own ground. We do not deny that a clever woman can equal or surpass an average man; nor that the present system of education is infinitely superior to the old dreary round of lessons. But even to that there are two sides. While girls are learning Greek and mathematics, they have little time for the needle-work, which used to be a part of every girl's education, and which they will want to understand at some period of their lives. It is the fashion now rather to sneer at darning, mending, and other trifling household duties; but if a woman is to be a wife and mother, she will need a good deal of such knowledge. It is a great thing to know the relation of one angle to another; but it is not every mathematician who brings her knowledge to a practical issue with regard to tables and chairs, or can tell whether a room has been properly dusted or not.

Woman was created as an helpmeet for man, not as his equal or rival; and woman nowadays is very apt to forget that fact.

In our life and country the little things are the woman's work; and many of our best and noblest women are those who spend their whole lives in trifles (not trifling). Little things—soothing a fractious baby, mending a husband's shirt, doing a little for the poor, caring for servants, keeping the household machinery oiled—

"Little things
On little wings
Bear little souls to heaven."

It has yet to be proved that Cambridge examinations assist women in their household duties, and one of the Oxford nonsense rhymes has a terrible significance in its inner meaning:

"'Who will marry you, my pretty maid?'
'Advanced women don't marry, sir,' she said."

VARIETIES.

SHORT-SIGHTED MORTALS.—When waves and trouble come over us, we say that troubles will never end; when God sendeth a fair wind, we think that the fair wind will never cease blowing.

NEW AND SECOND-HAND.
If thou wouldst tidings understand
Take them not at second-hand.

IN THE NEIGHBOURHOOD OF THE CAT.—People who have a strong antipathy to cats detect their presence by the odour, in circumstances which would be thought impossible. A lady in my study one day suddenly remarked, "There is a cat in the room." On my assuring her there was none, she replied, "Then there is one in the passage." I went out to satisfy her; there was no cat in the passage, but on the first landing-stairs, looking through the railings, sure enough, was the cat.—*G. H. Lewes.*

A GREAT INFLUENCE.
CHEMISTS tell us that a single grain of iodine will impart colour to seven thousand times its weight of water. It is so in higher things: one companion, one book, one habit may affect the whole of life and character.

Right: The Disadvantages of Higher Education, *an article by M.P.S., appeared in February, 1882. A few weeks later, in April, the Editor published an energetic reply by Bertha Mary Jenkinson, one of his teenage readers.*

The regular Varieties feature, an example of which follows M.P.S.'s article, covered a vast range of anecdotes, jokes, sayings and proverbs.

Far right: readers' verses, short stories, and essays were printed in The Girl's Own Page of Amateur Contributions. *Many compositions were sentimental, most predictable, but sometimes, as with Bertha Jenkinson's letter, they sounded a refreshingly individual note.*

AN OCCASIONAL PAGE OF AMATEUR CONTRIBUTIONS.

NOTE.

THERE are few habits so conducive to a well-regulated mind as the careful writing down of one's thoughts and sentiments in black and white, and our God-given power of influencing others for good is extended, if we are able to express ourselves clearly and correctly. These amateur compositions are inserted with a view to encouraging our girls in the practice of committing their thoughts and experiences to paper for the benefit of their sisters. Nothing thus printed is to be looked upon as perfect in composition, and the Editor wishes it to be understood that he will print only such verses or papers as shall be written in correct taste, interesting in subject to the general reader, and shall contain the age of the writer, and be certified as her *bonâ fide* work by a parent, minister, or teacher.

LIFE'S MUSIC.

Do the chords vibrate but lightly ?
　Or are they full and deep ?
Does the music murmur gently,
　Like a little child asleep ?

Or is it harsh and broken,
　Like moanings of the wind,
While we grow weary seeking
　A tone which we cannot find ?

There is a sweet note somewhere,
　If we could only see,
It would make a sweeter music
　And a fuller harmony.

Perhaps that note we're needing
　From others' life is caught ;
And its melody is answered
　In our own deep train of thought.

For everyone must perfect
　His work of love and life,
Must keep it purely spotless
　In the midst of sin and strife.

And there is One to help us,
　Who knows that we alone
Can never make it holy,
　Never purify its tone.

He takes our burden from us,
　And tells us in His love
Our life-work shall be perfect
　In Our Father's home above.

OLIVE HAWTHORNE (aged 15½).

DEAR MR. EDITOR,—The first remark I wish to make on the article entitled "The Disadvantages of Higher Education," by "M. P. S.,"* is, that it is unmistakably written by a man, and one who certainly has never had a wife who has been highly educated, or he would not have wasted his time in penning the article before mentioned. He says a woman's physique is not equal to that of a man's, and therefore the brain power of a woman can never equal a man's. That may be ; but is it necessary, does it follow that a woman after she has learnt to read and write, to sew, clean a house, and cook a dinner, should allow her brains to lie dormant ? I think not. A woman's education must go on all her life, exactly the same as a man's, or she will never be even a helpmeet for her husband.

If God had intended woman to be merely man's slave he would never have furnished her with reasoning powers. She need not have had even a tongue, for she could have cooked his dinner and mended his shirt quite as well without one. I think if such had been the case the emancipation of slaves would never have taken place. As for girls never learning sewing nowadays, I know that any girl educated in a Board School thoroughly understands the practical work of cutting out and putting together materials of all kinds.

Do you think, Mr. Editor, that "M. P. S." ever read Sidney Smith's "Pleasures of Knowledge"? If he did, I wonder if he skipped the following passages or read them :— "I appeal to the experience of every man who is in the habit of exercising his mind vigorously and well, whether there is not a satisfaction in it which tells him he has been acting up to one of the great objects of his existence? The end of nature has been answered : his faculties have done that which they were created to do ; not languidly occupied upon trifles, not enervated by sensual gratification, but exercised in that toil which is so congenial to their nature and so worthy of their strength."

This applies equally to a woman as to one of the other sex. There is an anecdote I have read which I think is appropriate to the subject in hand. It is as follows. "When I lived among the Choctaw Indians I held a consultation with one of their chiefs respecting the successive stages of their progress in the arts of civilised life, and among other things he informed me that at their start they made a great mistake—they only sent boys to school. These boys came home intelligent

men, but they married uneducated and uncivilised wives, and the uniform result was the children were all like their mothers. The father soon lost all his interest both in wife and children. "And now," said he, "if we would educate but one class of our children, we would choose the girls, for when they become mothers they educate their sons."

In THE GIRL'S OWN a few months since I read that God did not take woman from man's head, so as to be his superior ; nor from his feet, so as to be his inferior ; but from his side, in order to make her his equal and companion, and unless a woman is educated she certainly cannot be either his equal or companion.

But, Mr. Editor, I fear I am taking up your valuable space, so I will be contented with merely mentioning that some women cannot be wives and mothers. They have their living to earn and must go out in the world, and if they are not educated, and highly educated too, I think the right word to apply to them would be incapables. I infer from "M. P. S." that he considers all women's reasoning faculties are not alike. He says that " While the talented women of this generation are studying to equal men on their own ground, they are leaving the women's posts for the incapables." Now, all women are not geniuses, neither are they incapables. There are some go-betweens, and these are the ones fitted to be wives and mothers. I do not mean to say that a genius would not make a good wife and mother, but possibly her genius requires her to concentrate her whole energies on one object. Then the go-betweens ? They are improved, refined, and better able to train their sons to be great, good, and noble men, than if they had no sympathy with their tastes and feelings. A man enjoys talking to another, about politics for instance, and more so when he knows his opponent is "worthy of his steel." Would he not feel just the same pleasure in arguing with his wife, if she were educated, so that she could understand and talk sensibly and intelligently with him ? Then, again, a talented woman is not obliged to be a heathen. Possibly, indeed most probably, she will be an earnest-minded Christian.

"M. P. S." also says if a woman advances too far she will certainly fall. I say the same of a man, but a woman cannot advance too far if she be sure of every step she takes. I could say more, Mr. Editor, but will refrain. And now, with numerous good wishes to you and "Our Girls,"—I am, yours sincerely,

BERTHA MARY JENKINSON
(Aged 14 years and 7 months).

---

* M. P. S. is *not* a man, but the daughter of an illustrious dignitary of the Church of England.—ED.

THE GIRLS OF THE WORLD.
FACTS AND FIGURES.

Countries and Cities.	Girl and Women Population.	The Number of Defective among our Women and Girls.			The Number of Women and Girls professing the various Creeds.		
		Blind.	Deaf and Dumb.	Lunatics and Idiots.	Roman Catholics.	Protestants.	Other Christian sects.
England and Wales	13,334,537	10,784	6,831	44,714	531,250‡	11,429,375‡	27,792
Ireland	2,599,044	3,166	1,259	7,439	2,019,091	621,413	
Scotland	2,017,901	1,602	993	7,562	185,936	853,320	750,000
Victoria	428,720	240	119	1,286	102,836	238,976	10,711
New South Wales	368,126	No returns.			30,135	76,605	253
Queensland	102,660	No returns.		200	25,848	62,741	629
South Australia	138,174	75	90	288	20,757	97,224	9,516
West Australia	13,215	18	8	51	3,876	8,658	115
Tasmania	57,348	90	31	209	No returns.		
New Zealand	284,405	59	54	400	32,021	177,358	3,663
France	18,748,772	13,612	9,887	26,185	17,763,184	283,222	10,283
Italy	14,194,245	9,571	6,593	8,098	13,267,503	29,969	16,667
Switzerland	1,454,476	2,932	6,544		530,391	825,044	5,418
Spain	8,200,215	8,404	5,004	6,673	8,000,000	2,349	4,412
Austria	11,324,507	10,460	16,770	9,541	8,896,824	205,315	259,568
Hungary	7,939,197	8,621	10,074	9,855	4,734,909	1,699,865	1,026,229
Germany	23,048,698	29,113	14,499		8,629,708	12,126,769	3,801
Prussia	13,864,245	11,300	10,846	27,052	4,172,854	8,135,097	11,092
Saxony	1,527,475	761	757	2,686	38,192	1,448,328	2,404
Bavaria	2,705,868	2,050	2,112	6,135	1,776,564	689,555	2,629
Belgium	2,829,475	1,304	868	2,975	Nearly all.	6,500	
United States	24,636,963	22,180	15,311	79,175	3,580,562	Not yet arrived at any certainty	9,610
Canada	2,135,956	1,303	2,457	4,515	895,881	1,211,609	
British India	123,949,970	272,326	75,943	30,776	*	158,865	893,746
Sweden	2,372,613	1,813	1,887	4,375	271	2,150,222	112
Russia	39,194,838				3,466,980	2,209,003	†28,201,846
Denmark	1,091,679	672	511	1,098	880	898,109	408
Grand Duchy of Baden	804,944	343		2,047	496,775	273,785	2,938
London	2,018,807	1,663	897	3,331	24,045	306,500	
Dresden	93,310	106	104		6,270	11,270	803

* 91,998,993 Hindus, 25,760,440 Mohammedans, 1,647,706 Buddhists.
† Greek Church.
‡ These figures refer to the census of 1871, no religious census having since been taken in England.

Above: in 1885–1886, Emma Brewer contributed a series of articles on The Girls of the World, *quoting facts revealed by the "wonderful science" of statistics. "It turns the bright flash of its lantern into the most secret places of a life, whether it be of an individual or of a nation, revealing at once the dark unhealthy corners … improvement, light and health must of necessity result."*

The age of *gentility* it is to be hoped is passing away in England, and a healthy, vigorous life is coming in. No good work could, in the nature of things, be done by women who hid it away, and thought nothing did them so much honour as white hands and silk dresses. The abundant wealth of the country is no doubt largely responsible for this; men have made money so freely that there has been "no occasion" for the daughters to work, and those who have been less successful, have thought that they lost caste if their daughters did what their neighbours didn't, and, as in China, artificial restraints were resorted to, to keep the fair young things delicate and idle.… A man (using man in its widest sense of human being) who does not work, is like a chrysalis, unformed and unsightly, with the beauty in which Nature intended him to be clothed all folded up and undeveloped.

The series included comment on the medical profession, which was suggested as a possible career for the readers of the *G.O.P.* a comparatively short time after its members had grudgingly admitted women. Elizabeth Blackwell had put her name on the British Medical Register in 1859, by virtue of her American degree; Elizabeth Garrett had done so in 1869, by virtue of her Society of Apothecaries' licence; Sophia Jex-Blake, after both these means of entry had been barred, succeeded in doing so in 1877.

The objections which are urged to medicine as a profession for women [ran an article in *Work for All*] never seem to be felt when they desire to become sick nurses, although the one calling is quite as laborious as the other, and there are few of the objections which in fairness would not apply to the sick nurse.

The series ended with a plea for equal pay:

It should be remembered that the work of girls is, as it were, on its trial. If it be found to be inferior to that of men it is but just that it should be paid for at a lower rate, but if equal or superior, surely it should stand upon its intrinsic worth, and be paid for accordingly. Every woman who does what she undertakes to do in the spirit of the true workman, rejoicing in it and doing it to the very best of her ability, is a benefactor to her sex—nay, more, a true patriot.

S. F. A. CAULFEILD

New Employment for Girls by Sophia Caulfeild in 1891 included some original suggestions. Massage was one of these, and there were some odd comments on this:

Too much of the operator's vital energy and magnetism may be absorbed by the feeble yet too keen recipient; or the weakly operator may, on the contrary, draw from the patient all the little vital power she possesses.

It sounds so perilous one wonders that people risked it. Medicine, surgery, chemistry, midwifery and dentistry were mentioned, and particular reference made to India as a wide field for women doctors because of the difficulties for men in "zenana practice" (the custom of segregating women in separate apartments to which no man could be admitted); *Work for All* had made the same point earlier. One very novel example appeared.

MARGARET BATESON.

In the United States we find that a grist and planing mill is in the hands of a "Lady-Miller", i.e. Miss Addie Johnson, of West Virginia. She has studied mechanics sufficiently to "take down and put together an engine as well as any engineer in the country"; and she has worked her mill for the last three years. This is quite a new vocation, and it seems worth a notice.

Another enterprising American, "Mrs Clara McAdow, the mining millionaire", was cited in 1894, and said to be "by no means 'unsexed' by the days of struggle, and fatigue, and association in her labours with working men".

A significant note was sounded in an article on employment by Margaret Bateson in 1897, dealing with the question of a fair day's pay for a fair day's work, with particular reference to the middle-class girl:

Everyone must be familiar with the usual line of attack. It takes the form of an appeal to a girl's generosity and to her fellow-feeling for other girls. The individual girl is reminded that if she remains living at home tranquilly and quietly (for movement is itself expensive), she can just manage to subsist. Then why should she insist upon doing work for pay? It is sordid of her to wish it. Moreover—and it is at this point that our tender-hearted girl succumbs—she must infallibly deprive other girls of a wage who need it more.... There is no proof that the general stock of work is growing less. It needs little imagination to foresee that manufactures may increase greatly, that trade can be indefinitely extended, and that a demand for many services is only waiting to be formulated when the services are supplied. Indeed, what we term the "Woman's Movement" means, if we regard it from one point of view, the creation of many demands. Who is it, for instance, who employs the expert

THE GIRLS OF TO-DAY.

By ONE OF THEM.

During the last few years it has been the fashion for people of all sorts and conditions to busy themselves about us and our position; they have given their opinions of us very freely, they have discussed our capabilities, or rather incapabilities, together with our future prospects very much as though we were marionettes, without souls or brains or hands.

We have looked in vain among these opinions for some practical benefit to be derived from a study of them, but what we have noted is a sort of compassion for us that we should have been born into the world at all, and that our being here is a cruelty to our brothers and fathers; for if we are stupid, they must keep us, and if we are clever, we rob them of their situations, and must keep them; but that which hurts us most is the opinion that we are useless lumber in the dear old homes.

We beg to differ on every point: in the first place, we join heartily in the General Thanksgiving, and thank God for our creation and preservation as for great blessings, and this we do every day of our lives. And in the dear homes, however poor they be, we feel and know we have definite places, and that when we leave them, it will mean sorrow to the dear parents.

If any among us are idle, and a good many of us are credited with this disease, we are rebuked; if, on the contrary, we are industrious and earn an independent livelihood, we are abused for taking the bread out of our brothers' mouths.

If we do not work, we are told that we cannot make good wives; and if we do work, that we shall be unable to make our husbands happy because they want companions more or less frivolous when they have been at work all day. Alas! we should be thoroughly deserving of all the compassion showered upon us from time to time, if we were moved one iota from our steady purposes by all the conflicting advice and opinions offered us.

It is our determination not to be objects of compassion, neither will we be useless lumber in our homes, neither will we arrange our lives with the one purpose of entrapping men to marry us.

We did not ask to come into the world but were sent here by a loving Father, and whatever our position we are thankful for being here, otherwise we should have known nothing of a Heavenly Father's love and glory and majesty. We should not have known the meaning of being His children.

And as to our earthly parents, there are very few indeed who would be glad to get rid of us, be they ever so poor, and as a rule we feel so sure of their love and help that we should not believe it even if they themselves told us they wished we had never been born: but enough of this. The fact remains that we are born and that God created us male and female; and what is more, He created us with powers for a purpose, and He surely expects us to use them, otherwise our hands, our brains, our heads, our hearts, might have been omitted.

Are we to be sorry that it is now quite rare to find, among us girls, one that sits down all day reading novels with a pet dog in her lap which she from time to time caresses, or that a girl willing to work is deterred from it by the fear of lowering her position thereby?

We are convinced that work is good for us; we are better for it physically, mentally and spiritually. We are altogether happier for it, and we object to being compassionated for doing that which our talents fit us for.

No girl will be the worse for a little money in the Savings Bank, but it will go doubly as far if she has placed it there out of her own earnings and not out of her father's.

We look round upon many families we know, and wherever we see a girl petted and thought too pretty or too delicate or too anything else to work, she is invariably discontented and unhappy—and why? Because she is not fulfilling her mission in the world.

If, as people say, we are robbing our brothers of their work, it must be because we take more pains with the work and do it better than they. Therefore let them look to it.

There is work for everybody; if not in one way, then in another. A lady whom some of us know was once very rich, and when her husband died she found herself quite poor, and would have been obliged to live upon her friends but for one gift she possessed, and peculiar as it was, she resolved to use it. It was that of mending clothes and linen, which she could do beautifully. She made her position known to several families who gladly engaged her on stated days in the month from nine in the morning till six in the evening, and needless to say, she is proving the greatest comfort possible to mothers of large families. For some years now she has kept herself not only independent, but able to put by a little for old age or sickness, and no one thinks of looking down upon her because she is doing the one thing she knew she could do well. In the same way a clergyman's daughter deprived of means had to face the world for herself and little sister, and knew that no one could clean or trim lamps better than she. So she at once made this accomplishment known, and she is getting a very tolerable income in this way without any loss of self-respect.

Working does not make us less womanly or less helpful in our homes or less affectionate to our parents, or, depend upon it, God would not have given us the capacity and the ability to work.

Who is the strength and the brightness of the home—the busy or the idle girl? The one who uses her brains or the one who lets them rust?

If people will interfere with us at all, let them try to build us up in vigorous, healthful work, teaching us that however humble the work we do, we give it dignity by doing it to the best of our ability.

Many of us girls belonging to the so-called upper class are extremely clever in dressmaking and millinery. Should we not prove benefactors to the small tradesmen and servant classes, if we could take rooms in various parishes where they could bring their materials and get them made up prettily and cheaply? As it is now, their dresses and bonnets are in wretched taste and badly made, and at a sum greatly in excess of what they can afford.

We have come to the conclusion that we shall live better lives and longer lives if we work well and cheerfully at that which falls to our lot. The nation will be the better for our influence and example, and our brothers cannot and will not be content to smoke and dawdle away their time at clubs and music halls while we, their sisters, are earnestly working.

Looking at things all round, we come to the conclusion that there is plenty of work to do, not only for our fathers and brothers but for us girls also. Out of this work we will select that which we can do best, whether it be nursing, teaching, book-keeping, mending, lamp-cleaning, dressmaking, or anything else. At the same time we will endeavour to hold fast by those attributes of modesty, gentleness and patience which belong to good women, and while we enrich the home with our earnings, we will try to be its sunlight and its ornament.

Above: The Girls of Today, *a lively article published in December, 1899, when G.O.P. readers were looking forward to the new century.*

woman shorthand-writer? It is, in many cases, the woman-lecturer, the woman of business, or the woman-doctor.... And though in London and our large towns we are slowly waking up to the fact that the capacities of women of the educated middle and upper class are not wisely allowed to atrophy, the country at large still wastes much useful labour. In how many of our rural districts is there a trained nurse, much less a cottage hospital, with a nursing staff of women? In how many country places are educated women trying by their own practical exertions to unravel the farmers' and the labourers' problems; in how many are they idling through their days, or at best bicycling over the country to kill time—and simply because they believe paid labour to be wrong....

I regard a pound a week as the average beginning salary of the middle-class girl. To the girl who in the factory or the workshop is earning less, and by very hard labour, I have no need to appeal. My only word to her is one of inducement, to try, by superior training, by combination, by whatever fair means lie in her power, to win more adequate pay. But the middle-class girl should begin with £1 a week; if possible, of course, with more; certainly not with less. And here I may say that the stories which I hear of girls who destroy each other's chances of salary, by offering to do work for board and lodging only, or for a salary less than that offered, I regard much as I should some exhibition of cannibalism.

While the *Girl's Own Paper* advocated feminine usefulness and the worth of honest labour, the unsentimental, professional note of this article, and the mention of "combination" particularly, comes as something of a surprise. Even though by the eighteen-nineties women were being allowed into men's unions (having until then usually had to form their own), the *G.O.P.* at this time is not a publication one associates with trade unionism. Obviously the writer knew that a pound a week was far out of the reach of the average working girl; many working men did not earn as much.

In general the *Girl's Own Paper* avoided matters of political controversy, although it was prepared to inform its readers on the state of the law. In 1890 A Solicitor wrote on *The Married Women's Property Acts*, discussing the greatly increased rights of married women to property of their own. And by 1898, in a series entitled *Letters from a Lawyer*, addressed to "My dear Dorothy" and signed "Bob Briefless", readers received advice on a variety of legal matters ranging from insurance and investments (2% per annum on £50 left to Dorothy by her godmother), to how to draw up a Will.

In *Some Types of Girlhood*, under the sub-title "*The Political 'Sisterhood', or Our Juvenile Spinsters*", the indefatigable Sophia Caulfeild asserted in 1890:

Politics are by no means outside a woman's sphere of influence; and her work would grievously lack completion were she to exclude it from the list of the necessary items of a general education. But "stump oratory" may safely be regarded as quite beyond the limits of a woman's social work. What could be more revoltingly unnatural than the grim, ungainly spectacle of a woman haranguing a mob?—a woman engaged in exciting the passions of socialistic and unprincipled men; exciting them to deeds of violence and insubordination, instead of entering their homesteads in private as messengers [*sic*] of harmony and peace.

However, the author goes on to say:

Before concluding my description of the type so nicknamed, I must warn my readers that it has been very unjustly applied in a large proportion of cases. Those opposed to any reform as regards the work, the improvement, and general influence of the sex, seem to feel a mischievous pleasure in classing all such reformers under one and the same opprobrious designation.

Five years later, in an article entitled *Politics for Girls*, the author (Frederick Ryland) prophesied:

MELBOURNE QUAY OF TO-DAY.

Above: Melbourne Quay, from an article of July 4, 1891. The author, W. Lawrence Liston, described how men lined the quayside to welcome the families "whose futures they have pioneered in this vast country". (He was to be taken aback by the remarkable friendliness of fellow passengers on Australian trains.)

Features on colonial life appeared at intervals, and would-be emigrants sometimes wrote to the Editor for advice. "No girl should go out without a thorough knowledge of housework and housekeeping, even to washing and ironing clothes," he warned. The energy and industry of successful colonists were much praised.

It seems probable that before the girls who read this page grow into full womanhood, the Parliamentary franchise—that is, the right and duty of voting for Members of Parliament—will be given to women in the United Kingdom as it has already been given in some of the Colonies. Many of the most influential members of both our great parties—the Conservatives and the Liberals—are in favour of the change; and in all probability it will be carried into effect within ten or twelve years.

The seventeen-year-old girl who, in 1880, had envied her brother his *Boy's Own Paper* and been delighted to get her own magazine, would have been in her thirties when that article appeared, perhaps already introducing a new generation to the *G.O.P.* But not until her daughters were adults would the dream of votes for women become a fact.

Chapter Two

HEALTH AND BEAUTY

Health can make the plainest girl pleasant to behold, if her mind be pure and innocent. Health causes the rich blood to mantle in the cheeks, brings the gladsome glitter to the eye, brightens the complexion, gives music to the voice, a charm to the smile, litheness and vigour to the limbs, and sprightliness and grace to every motion. So if you have beauty and purity of mind combined with bodily health, it is indeed impossible you can be ugly.

Article by Medicus
(1884)

Above: one of the engaging cartoons which appeared on the correspondence pages of some early issues (May 21, 1881).

Nobody will be surprised to hear that there were no articles on mascara or lipstick for the Victorian readers of the *Girl's Own Paper*. Lip salves, cooling washes, perfumed cod-liver oil, or the "little elegancy" of rose glycerine for redness or sunbrowning, were permitted. But, as MARY A. was told in 1887, "On no account use powder; nor, still worse, paint! No sensible, modest woman should resort to such measures."

However, they had regular articles on health and beauty, and although health was a long way in front, beauty was not quite forgotten. These articles appear under the name of "Medicus"—pseudonym of Dr Gordon Stables, M.D., C.M., R.N. (Introduction, page 18). His first article, in 1880, is called *How Can I Look My Best?*

Happy is the girl, I say, who can take and enjoy a bath in pure cold, soft water every day of her life.... Avoid coloured and over-scented soaps. Another mistake is the use of too rough a towel, and this rough towel, I am sorry to say, is often recommended by people who know no better. A moderate degree of friction is all very well, but, dear me, you do not need to rub your pretty skin off.... But probably the most harmless of all cosmetics, and certainly the best, is wetting the face with May-dew—I'm not joking, gentle reader—and if you have to get up quite early in the morning to go and look for it, and have to walk a mile or two before you find any, all the better.

Shortly afterwards, in *Health and Beauty for the Hair*, Medicus says:

If you want to have a good head of hair you ought to cultivate a calm and unruffled frame of mind. Nervous, fidgetty folks seldom have nice hair....

Below: an early article by Medicus (January 7, 1882), summarising, in its description of Jeanie Smith, many of his favourite recommendations.

MAXIMS FOR THE NEW YEAR.

By MEDICUS.

"Look before you ere you leap,
For as you sow you're like to reap."
Old Play.

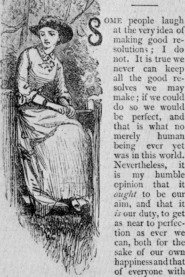

SOME people laugh at the very idea of making good resolutions; I do not. It is true we never can keep all the good resolves we may make; if we could do so we would be perfect, and that is what no merely human being ever yet was in this world. Nevertheless, it is my humble opinion that it *ought* to be our aim, and that it *is* our duty, to get as near to perfection as ever we can, both for the sake of our own happiness and that of everyone with whom we come into contact. You grant this; well, then, I'll tell you something. I mean this month not only to be your *Medicus* but your *Mentor* as well. Just for once in a way, you know, and I'm certain my fair young readers will forgive my presumption, for—it is a season of forgiveness. I would not be your accuser though, yet well I know that if you were to ask yourself this question, "Have I done all the good in my power for those around me and for myself in the year that is gone?" the answer would be expressed in a word of two letters instead of three. But, there, brighten up and read what I have to say; the year is young yet, the year is yours to do as you will with, and I would not have the hue of your resolution "Sicklied o'er with the pale cast of thought." No one, I may begin by telling you, who is not perfectly healthy can be truly happy and comfortable, and a person who is not both cannot bring joy to others, so that in resolving to do the best you can for your personal health, both mental and bodily, you are really consulting the good of others at the same time. That itself should in my opinion be inducement enough for any girl to learn and to try to abide by the common laws of health. But does obedience to these laws entail a very great deal of self-restraint and self-mortification? I do not think so, because good habits are just as easily acquired as bad ones. I pray you lay that to heart and remember, too, that—

"Ill habits gather by unseen degrees,
As brooks make rivers, rivers run to seas."

Besides, evil habits always bring wretchedness and misery in their wake, while good invariably lead to happiness and joy.

Now some of the hints and maxims regarding the care of the health, which I have embodied in my papers of last year, will bear repeating here in an epitomised form. But as I have very great objections to write anything in a dry tabulated kind of way, I will try to put before you what I have to say in the shape of a sketch.

The heroine of my little sketch I shall call Jeanie Smith, and I will try to paint you, from my imagination, just one day in her life. It is a very common, some might even say humble, name I have chosen for my heroine, and you cannot tell therefrom whether she be English, Irish, Scotch, or Welsh. But, whatever you do, don't imagine that Jeanie is a saint; she is neither more nor less a saint than any of my readers are. She has the same passions, good and bad, and the same temptations to do wrong instead of right, only, for the sake of illustration, I choose that she shall do what is right.

Jeanie's age is somewhere between ten and fifteen; she is neither rich nor poor, but she has duties to perform just the same as we all have. Jeanie lives in the country, but for all that she comes up to town sometimes in the season, and a year never passes without her having a holiday of some kind.

It is a clear frosty morning in January, with crisp crunchy snow on the ground, and the sun is shining quite brightly, although it is not much past seven o'clock. Jeanie wakes and rubs her eyes, and sits up in bed. She gives a little shiver as she does so. "Oh!" she thinks, "I do wish it were May or June once more, then early rising would not feel so hard." She would fain lie for only one little half-hour longer. It is a good thing she doesn't, for lying awake in bed of a morning is most enervating and depressing, but she remembers she has a little brother to dress, and several other household duties to perform, so she gets up within five minutes of the time she first opened her bright eyes. It is not good to spring at once out of bed; one ought to compose one's thoughts for a few minutes. This gives the heart time to prepare for the change, but do not take longer than five minutes, any more than Jeanie does. She kneels for a space of time beside her bed, and asks for guidance from Him whose guidance we all so much need.

Now the bath. The servant has brought a little hot water, to deprive the ordeal of its January chill. But it is still a cold bath. If it were not so, there would be no brace or tonicity in it. Tepid baths are only for bedtime. The glow produced by the bath—though not very great—is enough to give Jeanie heart and warmth to go on dressing. She even sings to herself as she does so, and this, by the way, is a sure sign that the bath has done her good. If young girls are healthy, they ought to want to laugh of a morning, and sing as the birds do. Jeanie's toilet adjuncts are all of the simplest, but good. Her tooth-powder is either charcoal or carbonate of soda, her tooth-brush is medium in thickness; her nail-brush strong and useful, like her little nail-scissors, which she does not forget to use. Thus Jeanie's teeth are like pearls, her hands are soft and white, and she never suffers from agnails. The soap she uses is mild transparent, the water *rain water*. Perhaps this accounts for the beauty and delicacy of her complexion, but only, mind you, to a partial extent, for Jeanie lives nearly all the day in the open air, and there is nothing in the world equal to fresh air, for not only beautifying but preserving the complexion.

Our heroine washed her hair some evenings ago, using warm soft water and yolk of egg instead of soap, so this morning it only needs well brushing to make it glitter like the wing of yonder blackbird, who is waiting for Jeanie to throw him his matutinal crumbs. A word about the bedroom itself. It is neat, and clean, and tidy, and everything is put in its place again as soon as used. Now the very fact of sleeping in such a room has an effect for good. A tidy apartment is a nerve tonic; an untidy one a nerve depressant.

But, see, Jeanie is dressed, and hurries away to perform her duties. She carries health with her, and that makes the duty seem light. Oh! what a holy thing is duty well performed. Duty! Have ever you studied the word in all its bearings?

Jeanie's is by no means a life of ease. I am sure she would not be happy if it were, nor half so healthy. Hours of leisure she has, of course, and these she devotes to exercise, to study, and to doing good. She always finds means of doing good, if only in a small way —to God's lower animals, for instance.

One of Jeanie's duties at meal times is to see that her little brother is properly served; that he doesn't eat too fast, and that he behaves himself like a young gentleman. It is good for her she has to do so, for thus her own food is not hurried down, and indigestion rendered impossible. The danger of eating too quickly is great, for the food is improperly masticated—it is not sufficiently mingled with the saliva, and too much is eaten, so the stomach is in consequence very greatly overtasked.

Jeanie has sewing to do as well as lessons to con, but neither at her needle nor at her books does she sit huddled up in an ungainly, cramped position. Indeed, she *never* sits thus; and her shoulders, in consequence, do not bend forward, nor is her spine bent, so she can walk erect; and as she never sews or reads in the dim twilight nor in strong sunshine, her eyes do not ache and her sight is as powerful as a bird's. She has learned that a great deal of work, whether sewing or reading, can be better and less laboriously performed out of doors than in; and much more pleasantly, too, because in the open air she is not only increasing her health, but learning to love life in every shape. Does she not see the flowers blooming around her, the trees gently waving their glittering leaves in the sunshine, and the bees at work, and does she not hear the birds singing? Ay, and Jeanie can sing, too, for well she knows how beneficial such exercise is, and how it keeps colds and coughs and consumption itself far away. She knows this, because "Medicus" told her; but even if he hadn't it would have been all the same, because it is as natural for a girl to sing, when healthy and happy, as it is for the lark.

Jeanie goes for a long walk, not after, but before dinner; but whether sitting or walking out of doors, she takes her mother's advice, and wears strong boots and warm stockings.

Here are a few truths or maxims about catching cold, which I throw in parenthetically. This climate being a most changeable one, it is advisable for every girl, especially if anywise delicate, to wear, winter and summer, flannel or silken underclothing, and woollen stockings or silken, with water-tight boots. Goloshes are bad. Pattens are excellent to wear about the doors in the country. In cold weather, while walking, wear a comforter; but loosen it if you feel warm. Do anything rather than sweat your neck. Don't sit in draughts, but do not be afraid of a good blow of fresh or even cold air. Avoid sudden changes from heat to cold; never go right away out of a warm room into a cold, to dress for an evening party. Thousands by doing so receive their death-blow. Avoid sitting in damp clothes; and if you get wet, don't be afraid of

Exercise greatly promotes the health and beauty of the hair. So does the bath. This latter should be taken every morning and as cold as can be borne.

EXERCISE AND THE BATH (Printer, put it in large type) [*sic*]. . . .

To ensure perfect cleanliness, the hair should be washed once a fortnight. Do not use soap; the yolks of two new-laid eggs must be used instead. The water should be rainwater filtered—lukewarm to wash with, cold to rinse out. Afterwards dry well and brush.

Exercise and the bath, sensible diet, and no tight-lacing are the usual lines of the advice given by Medicus. He is no advocate of "dosing" and says in one article, "To be a slave to aperient medicines is almost as bad as being a slave to opium" and in another, "If I had my will, I would clear out every bottle with a label on it from the nursery. Away with your syrups of senna and rhubarb, away with your still-waters, your slops and your oils." Girls brought up on Medicus's advice certainly ought not to have grown into mothers who gave their children a Friday-night dose of castor oil.

One of his early articles, in 1880, is headed *How To Be Healthy*:

Many girls between the ages of ten and fifteen suffer from what we medical men call anaemia, or, in plain English, poverty of blood. Such girls are often looked upon as merely delicate, and little that can be of any avail is attempted to be done for them. Here is a case in point, and it teaches a lesson that you will do well to lay to heart. Miss Julian A. is fourteen years of age; she is an only daughter and adored by her parents. But her mother says, expressively, "Julian won't make old bones." Her mother's words may come true, because this is the way in which she is treated: she is kept and coddled almost constantly within doors, she always has a little fire in her bedroom, and the window is seldom opened. If she goes out she is positively burdened with clothes, and, in addition to all kinds of good living, she is made to drink wine "to keep her up". She is pale and blanched in appearance, too weakly to work, and suffers from *back ache*. This case, and all others of the same kind, requires plenty

Above: in The Physical Education of Girls (*May, 1884*), *Mrs Wallace Arnold set out ten simple exercises with the chest expander ("procured at any surgeon's mechanist's or indiarubber warehouse"), to correct a stooping back brought about by study at desk, piano and drawing-board.*

Above: a description of the North London
Collegiate School for Girls (April, 1882)
praised its "gymnasium teas", when the
redoubtable Miss Buss invited her pupils to
merry tea-parties interspersed with spirited
games and gymnastic feats.

Far right: in his verses What Makes
Beauty?, the poet William Luff gives a
classic G.O.P. answer—sunshine.

"And so a common face grows fair,
If but God's sunshine glances there."

(October 12, 1889)

of exercise in the open air, the companionship of other girls of the same age,
good food, cod-liver oil, and tonics of iron.

And in *Why Am I So Pale?*, in 1890:

Bad meat and fish are expensive, and three times the amount of good blood
can be made from pea-meal, oatmeal, good bread, lentils, and mealy potatoes,
with a little butter and plenty of milk, for half the money. . . . In conclusion, let
me remind my readers of one lamentable fact; it is this—thousands of girls
suffer from paleness of countenance through tight-lacing. . . .

Tight-lacing is regularly denounced in the G.O.P.:

No adult woman's waist ought to measure less in circumference than twenty-
four inches at the smallest, and even this is permissible to slender figures only.
[1886]

Among the answers to correspondents in 1889 is the following:

MISS MONK inquires "how she may reduce" her natural waist from the size
which her Creator was pleased to make it, viz. twenty inches round, to sixteen
inches. We recommend her to apply at some hospital, and see whether she can
induce them to cut it open, and remove either some part of the liver or lungs
(as she could not very well dispense with her heart), and then she can have her
dresses reduced in the waist without stopping the action of the wonderful God-

created machinery inside. At the same time, we must frankly tell her that we could not form any idea of how long she would live with half a liver or half a lung. Apart from this question, we cannot imagine how anyone could wish to produce deformity.

It is not quite clear what a reader signing herself M. R. NORWOOD boasted of to merit the scolding she received in 1886, but it sounds rather like tight-lacing. She is told:

We pity you! To what a miserable, unwholesome state of deformity you have reduced yourself! We do not open our columns to persons who boast of having so far degraded themselves.

Although slimming is not condemned as firmly as tight-lacing, it is scarcely encouraged. DAISY is told in 1880:

[She] may be very thankful that she is blessed with such excellent indications of good health as the rosy face and a stout body. She must be very handsome indeed in face, and very unusually elegant in figure and in carriage, to look at all well if "thin". A thin little girl is a pitiable sight!

FLOSS in 1891 is told:

You will not benefit yourself by eating a lemon daily, nor trying vinegar, nor any plan of such a nature, to reduce fat. Probably you would succeed in thinning your blood, and your poor watery blood may develop dropsy, in lieu of good healthy fat. How would you like to become puffy and bloated?

Medicus does, however, admit that it is possible for a lady to become *too* stout. In *Health and the Toilet* (1890), after devoting some space to the problems of the scraggy lady, he writes:

Ladies, on the other hand, who are getting too rotund, should take time by the forelock. I can assure them that obesity, if it once commences, makes giant strides.... Avoid all oily and fatty foods, and all floury vegetables, cereals and sugar; take dumb-bell exercise daily, walk plenty; take a cold bath every morning; eat as little as possible.

The articles and the answers to correspondents in almost any present-day magazine for girls would have been inconceivable to Medicus or his Editor. The simplest gynaecological problems are absent from the pages of the *Girl's Own Paper*, and even bowels are decently referred to as "the system". One might not have expected corns to be unmentionable, but they are, or very nearly:

LADY CLARISSA has our thanks for her recipe for certain troubles connected with the wearing of tight, hard, or ill-fitting shoes; but of which (we find it requisite to tell our girls) no one ever speaks in "polite society". It is very vulgar to speak of them excepting in the privacy of a bedroom, and to a very intimate associate. However, we willingly give the recipe. "Mix some tallow and carbonate of soda very well together, and grease the painful supernumerary night and morning." We should suggest a nicer description of ointment than "tallow" as an adjunct to the soda. CLARISSA omits to name the proportions. [1887]

Beauty problems occur frequently in the answers to correspondents, but the replies tend to be brisk to a fault.

B.E.R.—We have answered both your questions over and over again. We can only now advise you to wear a veil, and keep your hands in gloves as much

Far right: an illustration from a serial by Ida Lemon (July, 1896), which makes a favourite G.O.P. point: beauty depends on the glow and sparkle of good health. Pretty as they are, sitting in their dainty dresses in a summer meadow, Kathleen and Dorothy would appeal whatever their garb and their setting, for they have the beauty of youth and health, charming manners and sweetness of expression.

"THEY HAD THE BEAUTY OF YOUTH AND HEALTH."

THE GIRLS OWN PAPER

LONDON

TWENTY ONE.

as possible. Neither disfigurement is always capable of cure. Red hands and freckles are natural to many. [1883]

SCOTCH THISTLE.—We are shocked to hear that you "never wash your face with soap"! The sooner you begin to do so, the better. Use soft water, or put some bran in it. Employ a mild, unscented soap at night, and then apply a little glycerine and water before drying it, or else, after drying, a little vaseline. In the morning, you need only bathe your face with cold water, as it will then be clean. It is the nature of some skins to shine. Wear a veil. [1884]

KATHERINE.—We congratulate you on having a colour. Too many girls look sadly washed-out, described so graphically in negro parlance as "poor catsy white trash". [1894]

FATIMA (Smyrna).—As to the dangerous attempt to give additional brightness to the eyes by artificial means, we greatly object to them. Some foolish, vain women employ belladonna—a drug that extends the pupil and injures the eye. . . . [1898]

An aristocratic correspondent in 1881, signing herself DAY-DREAM, is rebuked at once for two different kinds of vanity and for faulty syntax, as though to prove that the *Girl's Own Paper* stands in no awe of Debrett:

We are sorry to hear that you, a peer's daughter, are a perfect fright to look at with your red nose and fearful complexion! Your skin is naturally tender, and you have been using a too rough towel. Until that great entertainment at which you say you are to "come out", you should bathe the face morning and night in cold rain water, to which a little toilet vinegar has been added, and use cold cream at night. Your writing is good, but no better than it should be, for, with the advantages of having a governess to yourself, you *ought* to be a superior girl in everything. That you have yet to learn English is shown by your writing, "Will you please give a pattern of how to make a *woollen man's* glove in your paper?" We are not so well acquainted with the requirements of woollen men as we are with those of careless and boasting girls.

But some straightforward beauty advice does appear unaccompanied by moralising, as in the answer to BLANCHE in 1880:

At your age you need not be alarmed at your hair getting thin; it is probable that your system is a little out of order. Attend to your health; eat and drink nothing that stimulates or heats the system; take a teaspoonful of cream of tartar now and then of a morning. Use a hard brush for five minutes every day, morn and night, and the following stimulating pomade. Go to a respectable chemist and tell him to mix you two drachms of Wilson's stimulating ointment in an ounce and a half of nicely-scented pomade. Rub a little of this well into the roots of the hair every day, and wash once a week with juniper-tar soap, or mild carbolic acid soap.

In 1884 an exasperated Editor replies to MISETOE MAGGIE:

We have already announced to our correspondents that we have ceased to answer questions respecting the hair, the complexion, cosmetics, personal defects, blushing, and nervous shyness. Read what we have said about them before.

But by 1896 the Editor has relented at least to some extent:

AMY.—The use of curling-tongs is decidedly bad for the hair. While young it is not of much consequence, as the singed, dried up, and broken hair is renewed again; but this is not so in older women. The hair naturally becomes

Far left: Twenty One, *a portrait by Maria Stanley, published in the Annual of 1885–1886. The sitter, with her fresh complexion, simply dressed hair and loose white gown, adorned by just one rose, has the charm of good health and quiet manners so constantly praised by G.O.P. writers.*

Number 2 is less of a nuisance than an eye-sore. She is dressed to the waist as a man; thence, as divided skirts have not yet become fashionable, she necessarily remains a woman, at least in costume; in motion she yet strives to represent a man. This figure provokes one to laughter, calling to mind as it does that hybrid, the mermaid, which was neither fish, flesh, nor fowl, nor good red herring.

Again, what is more tiring than that mincing step so many affect, and what more tiring to the walker?

One more, the 5th—the girl who carries herself too well—that is to say, who pulls her shoulders back until it appears she could fall backward at a touch; the body is perfectly rigid; all the work is done from the hips downwards, which is manifestly not right. What does a doctor tell you about walking? It is the best exercise possible *because* it brings into play *all* the muscles of the body.

The natural movement is always the more graceful, and the beauty of motion is the ripple of the whole form, the beautiful sway of a beautiful line. The wonderful construction of the human body is expressed best in walking, each muscle giving and taking its share in the work.

"WITH BODY BENT FORWARD."

Above: a cartoon from an article on deportment by An Artist (May 9, 1891) in which the author caricatures particular faults of carriage.

Far right: Our Girls A-Wheel, *an energetic group, published in October, 1896.*

thinner and is not replaced in the same way when injured, and the natural oil not so efficiently supplied when dried up. The consequence is shown in partial baldness. Curling in soft paper is more prudent, and the curl looks more natural.

The hair, the complexion, cosmetics, personal defects, blushing and nervous shyness; all very familiar subjects of queries by the present-day teenager. It is perhaps hardly surprising that the G.O.P. readers took little notice of editorial admonition. FLORENCE MABEL in 1886 still has to be told:

The use of any kind of powder to the face is foolish and injurious, and is sure to be regretted at a future time, as it makes the skin coarse.

VIOLET, in the same year, is told:

We sympathise with you, and are sorry to hear of your "wrinkles" at nineteen; but we think you give too much attention to your face in the glass to be happy or barely contented. The wrinkles are probably caused by the sun and strong light. You must wear a veil, and bathe the face with oatmeal-water instead of soap. But do not mind your face so much; cultivate your mind and heart, and then you will be pleasant in everyone's eyes, even if plain in early youth and more deeply wrinkled still in extreme old age.

ABRUPT, writing in 1889, receives a reply which matches her pseudonym:

We cannot give you any recipe for making your hair grow dark, nor any for "getting rid of a double chin". Be thankful that you have got any hair or chin at all, and that the hair you complain of does not grow on your chin . . .

——one wonders whether ABRUPT continued a subscriber.

O.P.N. in 1891 is informed:

[She] need not feel worried at having a little down on her lip. If of a dark complexion it is very usual, and is not disfiguring, if slight, in the opinion of many; and you cannot expect *everyone* to admire you. Those who really care much for you would not wish to change any little special characteristic that marked the individuality of the face they loved.

One mysterious reply is addressed to PA'S DARLING in 1880, in which she is told to "rub the eyebrows three or four times a day with a piece of raw onion; you must not redden the skin, however". What was the raw onion intended to do, I wonder? To darken the eyebrows, to make them thicker or thinner? And did it work?

The articles by Medicus are most frequently concerned with general health matters—*When Not To Take Medicine* (1887); *Poverty of Blood: It Cause and Cure* (1888); *Shall I Ever Get Well, I Wonder?* (1889). Once in a while, however, he becomes more frivolous; in *The Toilet Table and What Should Lie Thereon*, he gives a recipe for tooth-powder which sound nasty:

Charcoal is unsightly but very effective, and it can be made more so by rubbing up with an ounce of it as much quinine as will lie on a sixpenny piece; a few drops of otto of roses may be added.

Recipes for cosmetics appear sometimes, as in *Lissom Hands and Pretty Feet* in 1880:

Here is a little bath for the hands, for which I am sure you will feel grateful. It is easily prepared, and if the hands are soaked in it for about ten

IN THE PARK.

HEALTH.

By GORDON STABLES, M.D., R.N. ("MEDICUS").

OVER-EXCITEMENT.

Would you be surprised to learn that this is very deleterious to the health of young ladies, and I don't care what the excitement may be, it has always to be paid for. Some girls are by nature finely-strung and emotional, and these have all the more need to take care of themselves. Even sentiment or what is called romance leads to emotionalism, and this in its turn to nervousness or even hysteria, and often to dire results.

I speak truly, I believe, when I say that your over-romantic, over-excitable and emotional girl is never likely to be married. Nor is the girl who is wanting in self-respect in so far as to be carried away by her feelings at any time. Therefore, I say, let girls have more solid exercise in the form of gymnastics or even athletics, and less reading of trashy suggestive novels, and less of the "moonlight on the sea" business. It may be that marriage is the goal that most young women try to reach, but they need not always be thinking about it, and the girl who looks upon every young man she happens to be introduced to as a possible suitor, generally conducts herself in such a way as to frighten that young man off, be he ever so eligible.

LOVE AND MARRIAGE.

There can be no continued happiness in married life if the marriage is not for love, and that, too, love on both sides. And if there be not compatibility of temper and tastes, love will evaporate. Of course there is true love and imaginary. I don't think that anyone tastes of the former more than once in a lifetime. Again love at first sight is a mere myth. True love can no more be built up in a day than a battleship can be built in a month, and don't you forget that, girls, please.

I heard an expression the other day which I did not quite understand, though I guessed its meaning. Two old ladies were yarning about a young lady, and said the one to the other, "She just threw herself at his head." Well, I am a fisherman, and that is not the way I should attempt to catch a *salmo ferox*. And really there is a good deal of the *salmo ferox* about every marriageable young fellow who is worth looking at. He is possessed of splendid strength, and has a fair share of the beauty of manliness, but he has a shy kind of wildness about him also, not unmixed with suspicion, and, like the *salmo ferox*, he is easily frightened away if the bait goes in with a splash right in front of his nose. "No, thank you," he thinks to himself, and swims off to look for something less easily obtained.

GIRLS AND THE CYCLE.

I have been an ardent cyclist all my life, and am but little likely to run the wheel down.

A lady-writer says, "The bicycle is the greatest emancipator for women extant—women who long to be free from nervousness, headache and all the train of other ills. The wheel stimulates the circulation and regulates the action of the digestive canal, thus driving away headaches, and as a cure for nervousness it stands unrivalled. In every motion which the rider makes, the muscles are brought into play and gently exercised. With head and shoulders erect, those of the chest and arms are given a chance, while the pedal motion gives ample play to those of the legs."

WHAT ABOUT EMANCIPATION?

That is the only word I take objection to in the above quotation. It sounds to a man's understanding as if women had hitherto been kept in disagreeable subjection to the stronger and sterner sex. I don't think any woman, unless an old maid, hankers after emancipation of that sort, which seems to mean that, mounted on her bike, a girl can ride away anywhere and do anything all alone, without either male friend or chaperon, that she can guide and protect herself and be as free and easy as the wind. Well, I can assert, without fear of contradiction, that no man can really and truly care for a girl of this independent character, nor of one who pretends she can do everything manly quite as well as a man, only more so. Who wants a woman with a biceps, anyhow? Such a one is usually deficient in the gentler arts of her sex. Your women who scull much, or golf or hockey a deal are usually coarse in skin and in features, and far indeed from beautiful. No, girls, don't let us have too much of that emancipation business. Better to be loved and admired by a true and good man than be "emancipated."

BUT CYCLING MAY BE ABUSED.

There are times when no girl should cycle much. At any other time an hour's spin, so long as she does not race, is most delightful, provided the roads are good and the machine in order. In this case you have no occasion even to envy the swallows. But if instead of enjoying the scenery and the fresh air, you only try how far and how fast you can go, ten to one the run will do you little good and may do incalculable harm. Listen: every human being on earth has some organ or portion of the body that is weaker than the rest. It may be the lungs in some, the liver in others, or—so on and so forth, but it is on this weak organ that the strain of fatigue works its worst.

See that you have the best saddle that can be procured, and that you do not have to stoop. Ride in your very easiest corset, compatible with a figure free from actual dowdyism—I assure you I don't want you to look ungraceful, but health is the first consideration, isn't it? You will find riding from home less fatiguing than coming back, but all the same you have to return, so take care not to tire yourself out. The weakly should never ride on an empty stomach, nor after a full meal.

SLOW DIGESTION.

This is a complaint that very few girls are subject to. But it does occur sometimes, and it should not be put

minutes morning and evening in summer, it tends to keep them nice and white and free from roughness. You put a pinch or two of powdered alum and a teaspoonful of powdered sal ammoniac in about a pint and a half of warm salt water, and dissolve; then, when you have added a little toilet vinegar, this elegant hand bath is ready for use.

In 1886, in *Toilet Table Elegancies*, readers are told:

Lard 4 ounces, white wax $\frac{1}{4}$ ounce, alum in powder a teaspoonful, and a little alkanet to colour, make a beautiful and useful lip-salve. If you add to it a few drops of otto of roses, you have indeed an elegant preparation.

More recipes appear in *Rational Toilet* in 1892:

What is called virgin's milk is made by taking, say, half a pint of rose water and adding thereto three drams of Friar's balsam. This is an excellent and simple face cosmetic. Here is a wash for sunbrown or freckles; but although it is cooling as to sunbrown, I could not vouch for its efficacy in freckles. It is made with one dram—that is, one ordinary-sized teaspoonful—of California borax, 4 ounces of lime juice, and about two teaspoonfuls of candy sugar. Put all these together and mix well; then add a little eau de cologne.

It would be nice to know how many readers were tempted to experiment with these recipes; or with those given in 1898 (not under the name of Medicus) for Oriental Face Cream, Hair Restorer and Bloom of Roses—a somewhat more sophisticated note appears to be creeping in with these.

In *How To Look Well in the Morning* (1892), Medicus writes:

Perfumed cod-liver oil may be rubbed well in around the eyes before lying down. This may not seem a very fascinating way of treating coming wrinkles, but it is often an effective one, for in this way the tissues under the skin are nourished to some extent, and kept full. Face massage may also be used.

In the same article readers are told:

The peculiar diathesis that leads to the formation of these black-heads often leads also to the secretion of acid, or so-called sour perspiration; and people who suffer from either ought, in the first case, to regulate the diet. Drink warm milk instead of tea. Drink hot or warm milk with dinner and supper in preference to anything else. Take a glass of hot water some time after breakfast with a few drops of lemon juice in it. The bath daily in some form is absolutely necessary.

In *Beautiful Hands* in the same year, Medicus says:

The liquor of boiled oatmeal groats will tend to whiten the skin; but it must be made fresh every day—it won't keep. A cocoa-nut oil liniment is sometimes used to rub into the hands at night to whiten them. It is composed of half an ounce each of cocoa-nut oil, white wax, and almond oil, nicely scented.

Oatmeal is recommended again in the reply to JESS in 1888:

Many people who cannot use glycerine or vaseline for their hands in the winter, find great benefit from oatmeal and honey; mixed, and rubbed into a smooth paste. This is put on the hands when they are washed, and proves healing to many skins that grease does not help. Oatmeal alone may also be used, instead of soap, when washing the hands.

Another homely hint in 1892 is "an old-fashioned but good" remedy to clear a complexion from "muddiness":

Far left: some twenty years after his first articles on health for the G.O.P., Medicus is still writing in his incomparably personal style (August, 1901), although The New Doctor now contributes occasional, and much staider, articles to the magazine.

Above: among these Miscellaneous queries of January 22, 1887, are a number of the usual appeals, all answered in the usual uncompromising fashion.

To a pint of filtered rain-water add a wineglassful of lime juice and a few drops of attar of roses. Shake well. To use it you simply damp the face and hands with it, and let it stay on for a few minutes. This may be done three times a day.

As the *Answers to Correspondents* (Chapter 9) indicate, vanity was not encouraged in the *G.O.P.* Medicus writes in 1883:

The very first signs of a love of outré finery in a child-girl should be checked by the mother; older girls should check it in themselves, as they would the thought of a deadly sin. It often leads to the utter ruin of all correct deportment in society, and causes the girl to be looked down upon even by people of both sexes.

It is curious to turn from the beauty pages in modern magazines for girls, dealing with moisturiser, tinted foundation, blusher, powder, eye-shadow and the rest, to an article called *Beauty* by Medicus in 1888:

Health is the true basis of all female beauty. I have an observing eye, and make good use of it. Well, I declare to you that when I meet young ladies rouged, powdered and pencilled, I wonder if the world is getting worse. For deceit thus carried about openly can have no good effects on the moral character. Many girls moving in what is called good society, a sadly mixed compound nowadays, are little better than walking frauds, perambulating fibs. I will not put it any stronger, but I can let my imagination whisper to me what some of these "angelic beings" look like in the morning before they are ready to emerge from their rooms.

I would not speak so plain, I would not hit so hard, if I had not a remedy to suggest. To those girls, then, who think they are adding to their beauty by the use of cosmetics, I would say, "There would not be any occasion to use such abominations if you would attend to your health."

"My skin is not so clear as it should be," someone says, and she forthwith powders it, adding, perhaps, a tint of carmine to the lips and a little pencilling to the eyebrows; and lo! she is transformed. Yes, but very transparently so. "A thing of beauty is a joy for ever." But not in this case. This made-up girl will not be a thing of beauty after she is twenty-one, and younger girls not made-up, but happy and joyous with the true beauty of health, will laugh and call her "an old thing" when she is not within hearing.

To obtain this true beauty of health Medicus recommends restricting the diet, with more vegetables, fewer rich dishes and sauces, no stimulants, early rising, a Turkish bath once a week or a hot bath twice in ten days, a well-ventilated room with plants in it, "The Girl's Own Bath" every morning (a quick wash all over with hot water and the mildest transparent soap, followed by a cold sponge tub with a couple of handfuls of sea-salt), and as much exercise as possible.

Writing many years later, in 1898, the same author says:

There is nothing that some females will not do or suffer for the sake of being considered pretty or beautiful. There are places in London where they pretend even to excise or stretch out wrinkles and crows' feet about the eyes and give the simple semi-idiotic patient—they need to be patient—an entire new skin.

Chapter Three

FICTION
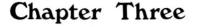

Who is wise?	She who learns from everyone.
Who is powerful?	She who governs her passions.
Who is rich?	She that is content.

Wisdom, Power, and Riches
(1890)

During the period under review, each issue of the *G.O.P.* included instalments of two serial stories; these instalments were usually quite short, but the serials frequently ran for months. They were not particularly juvenile in style or content. Heroines below marriageable age were few and most of the stories could have been read quite as happily by a granny in search of a light novel as by one of the teenagers for whom they were officially written. It would be going too far to say that all these serials were "improving", but not that the moral effect of even the lightest was taken into consideration.

On the first page of the first number in 1880 is the beginning of the first serial: *Zara: or, My Granddaughter's Money* by an anonymous author. The plot, rather more highly coloured than many which followed it, begins with an old woman spending a night in the lodging-house run by the mother and stepfather of the hero, Paul, then a child; she confides in Paul's mother that she is searching for her granddaughter, Zara Meldicott Keith, from whose mother she has been estranged and to whom she intends to bequeath her money. She leaves a bag in the care of Paul's gentle mother when she goes, and the reader is told that shortly afterwards she collapses and dies. Eventually Paul's stepfather insists on opening the bag in Paul's presence and discovers it to contain a fortune which he takes for himself, swearing the frightened child to secrecy. Before Paul's mother dies, she charges her son to make restitution to Zara Meldicott Keith if he ever discovers her. Not long afterwards the stepfather dies and leaves the money to the boy. We pass over a period of many years, at the end of which Paul is a medical student, attached, though not yet engaged, to a charming and suitable girl. Then by chance he sees a music-hall poster bearing the unforgettable name of Zara Meldicott Keith, and his mother's words return to him. At the music-hall he sees her:

THE GIRL'S OWN PAPER

VOL. I.—No. 1.]   JANUARY 3, 1880.   [PRICE ONE PENNY.

ZARA:

OR, MY GRANDDAUGHTER'S MONEY.

CHAPTER I.
AN ARRIVAL.

THE streets of a dreary London suburb were more dreary than usual on that December evening. A dense fog was fast gathering up its yellow vapour, making the shabby, tumble-down region only one degree less obscure than it would be at mid-night. Jasper Meade, proprietor of the "Commercial Lodging House," stood on his own door-step, whistling a dismal refrain very much out of tune, but at the moment he was not thinking of melody — his keen, restless black eyes were striving to penetrate the mist. He watched every vehicle that rattled past, splashing through the sloppy mud, waking up the echoes for a short space, and disappearing into the obscurity beyond, and considered it another lost chance, a fresh disappointment. The secret of this was that Jasper's last venture in the world of speculation was not realising his expectations.

He had lately purchased the lodging-house before-mentioned, and found his venture was of questionable advantage. It had been described in the advertisement as "ruinously cheap," having

"WILL YOU COME TO MY LITTLE ROOM?"

spacious, well-furnished rooms, good stables, every convenience for man and beast, and doing a splendid business. Tempted by the delusive bait, he had rashly invested the whole of his capital in the purchase, awakening too late to the knowledge that much gloss and rosy tint is apt to be used in advertising, and that a bargain rarely comes up to the description given of its merits.

Rooms, many and various, there certainly were in the old house, but they looked as though generations of bygone travellers had tarried there, disported themselves without restraint, and then gone on their ways. The walls were sullied and grimy, the furniture worn out, the carpets ragged and faded, the whole place disreputable in the extreme. Jasper's wife — a pretty, bright-eyed little woman, charming with her Frenchified manner, born and bred a lady — had been driven to utter despair when Jasper took her down to that suburban establishment, and told her it was to be their future home! The meanness and vulgarity of the place were repugnant to Phillis; every instinct of her nature revolted, she

A mere child in years—little more than seventeen, who ought still to have the timid bashfulness, the sweet, delicate, blossoming freshness of early youth —shrinking from aught that was forward, obtrusive, and conspicuous. Yet there she stood, unabashed, in the full glare of the footlights, looking assured, confident, self-reliant as a woman of twenty-eight might have been. And men were clapping at her, and boys were stamping their feet at her in wild applause.

Afterwards Paul goes to see Zara, and is filled with remorse because she has grown up without the advantages of education her grandmother's money could have given her, advantages which that same money has given him. But he believes that to present a friendless girl of seventeen with a fortune would cause worse problems than leaving her in her present position, and his attempts to befriend Zara are, not surprisingly, misconstrued. The only thing he can think of to do is to give up any thought of his former sweetheart and marry Zara as a means of restitution. This plan, going beyond quixotry into imbecility, causes trouble to everybody concerned. Mercifully, Zara resolves the problem by returning to a former suitor and emigrating with him, receiving her fortune as a wedding present from a thankful Paul.

In *The Follies of Tressida* (Anonymous, 1884), two sisters have a double wedding. Coquettish Tressida is thought fortunate in securing "the finest

Above: the concluding episode of The Follies of Tressida (*March, 1884*), *when one look at Tressy's despair convinces Susan that her sister has done wrong. "What a wicked girl I am!" cries Tressy.*

Far left: the first episode of the anonymous serial Zara, *which opened the first issue of the magazine in 1880.*

57

Above: an excursion for Margaret Stewart, heroine of A King's Daughter, *in the days when "the sun was still shining" for her; in the party are the worthy local minister and Margaret's protégée, May Castle.*

Right: an unusual short story, Weaving the Dusky Strand, *appeared in the G.O.P. on September 15, 1888. Set in India, it is a rare example of the dramatic adventure story, so common in the pages of the* Boy's Own Paper, *the G.O.P.'s brother publication.*

young fellow in Barstowe", while doubts are expressed over the choice, by her steady sister Susan, of a man who used to be "too fond of a drop". Once married, Susan spends her spare moments reading the cookery book and reaps a harvest of domestic happiness, while Tressy sits among the unwashed dishes reading *On the Way to a Coronet*, feeds her husband on bread and cheese, lives beyond her income, and ends by driving him to drink and herself to dishonesty. Her husband, crying, "She'll make a drunkard of me if I stay with her any longer. Curse her! I was a fool to marry her!" disappears for three years, at the end of which he returns to a repentant and reformed wife.

Some of the stories in the *G.O.P.* are of a sober nature. In *A King's Daughter* (Isabella Fyvie Mayo, 1884) there are two heroines, the queenly young Margaret Stewart, daughter of a Shetland laird and engaged to a marquis, and May Castle, a foundling, owing her name to the fact that she was discovered in the ruins of a castle in the month of May. May is

making all who are guests like yourselves wish for a similar meeting, and remember with pleasure the one that is past.

In giving invitations, if you wish your visitors, whether few or many, to be happy, bestow some thought on the elements which are to compose your party. Think whether they will be glad to meet each other; consider in what amusements they have shown an interest, what are their tastes and accomplishments, and how you may best turn these to account for the general good.

A chemist who was combining various ingredients would not put in an extra one which would set all the rest in a ferment, merely for the sake of filling up the vessel which contained them. So let me advise you, dear girls, never to spoil your party for the sake of filling up a seat or giving what may be deemed a "duty invitation," in order to pay a social debt. And let all understand beforehand just the kind of gathering in which they are to take part. In my next chapter I shall endeavour to suggest some ways of entertaining your friends when they are met together.

(*To be continued.*)

MARGARET TRENT, AND HOW SHE KEPT HOUSE.

By DORA HOPE.

"How nice and soft and thick your stair carpets are, Margaret," said Dorothy Snow to her friend as they went upstairs together. It was a week or two before Christmas, and Dorothy had come to spend a long day, to take advantage of Margaret's proximity to the London shops. "It gives me a most luxurious feeling, suggesting velvet pile and that sort of thing, which one does not expect on a staircase," she went on.

"I expect yours are the same, only that my pads being new are perhaps more noticeable."

"Pads!" Whatever have they to do with it?" asked Dorothy.

"Oh, don't you know that it is such an advantage to have a pad on each stair, under the carpet? We used to have an old stair carpet instead, at home, which does almost as well; but in our new house of course we had no old ones, so the upholsterer put down these pads. They make the carpet feel and look much thicker, and save the wear a good deal too; I have a great objection to threadbare stair carpets, but they require a great deal of care to prevent them becoming shabby; I have them moved about an inch either up or down every week. Perhaps you are not aware that stair carpets are always bought rather longer than is absolutely necessary to allow of moving them about, and the surplus piece is either hidden under another carpet, or turned under, according to circumstances."

"Oh, yes, I did know that. At any rate, I am constantly falling headlong downstairs, and then being scolded for my carelessness in not noticing that the rods were out, and the carpets being moved."

"Well, there is nothing like an experience of that kind for fixing a fact in one's mind," rejoined Margaret, laughing. "Now I think I shall have time to try an experiment on these wax candles before we go out. I am rather anxious about them, for Aunt Annie gave them to me; she was going to use them up in the kitchen, as being too dirty and discoloured for anything else, so I begged them, as I thought I could whiten them by rubbing with flannel dipped in spirits of wine."

"Did you invent that, Margaret?"

"Oh, no. Somebody or other told me about it, but I have had no opportunity to try it before."

Margaret's aunt, being country born and bred, had hitherto had a strong prejudice against gas, and had used nothing but lamps and candles in her house. At last, the superior cheapness and convenience of gas had overcome her scruples, and she had submitted to it; at least, so far as the halls, kitchens, and bedrooms were concerned. She refused, however, to have the large ugly gaseliers hanging from the centre of the ceiling, and instead had branch lights from the walls, in various convenient spots, by which arrangement it was possible to read or work comfortably in any part of the room.

"IT'S ENOUGH TO MAKE A MAN TURN BURGLAR."

proud and sensitive, loved by nobody except her cat. The marquis shows his fiancée May's paintings, and Margaret invites the girl for a holiday in Shetland. Scarcely has the visit begun than it is discovered that Margaret and her parents have even less claim to the name of Stewart than May to that of Castle, since Margaret's grandfather had fraudulently passed off his own son as the heir to the property. Margaret's delicate mother dies suddenly before learning the truth, and very shortly afterwards the legal owner of the property, an American, arrives in Shetland with his vulgar wife and daughter. Then Margaret's fiancé, the marquis, is drowned leaving the island. Chapter XXI ends:

And that was the last that was ever seen of the bright, beautiful young Margaret, mistress of Balacluva. Next morning——

(*To be continued.*)

Chapter XXII, *After the Storm*, opens:

Next morning, Margaret came out of her room, a pale woman, with a strain across her brow and a strange light in her eyes. Her youth lay behind her. She had served God hitherto in her days of triumph and happiness and love; and whatever else was changed, He remained, though she must serve Him henceforth in solitude and patience and faith.

At the end of the story the foundling May is a distinguished painter, married to a man she met in Shetland. Margaret is living with her father, now feeble-minded, and a widowed friend, supporting herself by teaching.

She was still God's lady, though she had ceased to be the lady of Balacluva. A King's daughter does not lose her royal lineage because it is her Father's will that she should be "all glorious" only within and not without.... A story which ends by leaving a soul at the gates of heaven cannot be "a sad story". We need pity no one who has proved her birthright as "the King's daughter".

Our Bessie (1888), by the very popular and prolific Rosa Nouchette Carey, is in a lighter vein. Bessie is a typical *G.O.P.* heroine, simple, modest, sensible and bright. The theme of improvement is a favourite one in *G.O.P.* fiction; sometimes it is the principal character herself who is in need of it, while sometimes she effects it in others. In *Our Bessie*, the improvement takes place in the rich young lady Edna Sefton, whom Bessie meets when their train is held up in the snow. As a result of this meeting, she spends a holiday with Edna, her mother and stepbrother. During this period the spoiled Edna loses her fiancé as a result of her caprices, and Bessie grows to love the stepbrother, who has been starved of affection. Eventually Edna gains wisdom and humility, and regains the fiancé, while Bessie marries the stepbrother. The story is basically a sunny one, but has its pathetic side in the life and death of Bessie's young sister Hatty, who suffers not only from poor physical health but from a fretful, difficult and depressive temper which she struggles to conquer. Bessie says to her:

We can't make ourselves good, Hatty; that lies in different hands. But why don't you look on your unhappy nature as your appointed cross, and just bear with yourself as much as you expect others to bear with you? Why not exercise the same patience as you expect to be shown to you? ... Why don't you say to yourself, "I am a poor, weak, little creature, but my Creator knows that

ISABELLA FYVIE MAYO

Far left: Dora Hope's series Margaret Trent and How She Kept House *appeared in 1882, following on from an earlier series featuring Margaret before her marriage to Wilfred Trent,* The Difficulties of a Young Housekeeper and How She Overcame Them. *Domestic advice is pleasantly disguised as fiction in the description of the young couple's establishment. Here the local constable, after disturbing a burglar at work, gives Wilfred good advice on securing the windows at night.*

ANNE BEALE.

RUTH LAMB.

too, and He bears with me. I cannot rid myself of my tiresome nature; it sticks to me like a Nessus shirt"—you know the old mythological story, Hatty—"but it is my cross, a horrid spikey one, so I will carry it as patiently as I can. If it is not always light, I will grope my way through the shadows; but my one prayer and my one effort shall be to prevent other people suffering through me"?

Another sunny story is *A Lonely Lassie* by Sarah Tytler (1891), dealing with the adventures of the seventeen-year-old orphan daughter of a Scottish country minister who comes to live in London with her fashionable relations. Scots heroines seem to appear to *G.O.P.* writers as essentially simple, reliable, and strictly virtuous, and here the rustic Flora is a thoroughly practical and sensible little soul, determined to hold to her childhood values in her new life. Her aunt wishes her to overcome her unmistakably Scotch accent, and Flora is hurt:

… A hundred times more hurt than if her red cheeks, which she could not defend, the fashion in which she dressed her hair on the top of her head, that her father had liked, the manner in which she disposed of her hands, or sat on her chair, had been attacked simultaneously…. Her protest was addressed to herself, and to no other. "Of course I shall try not to say Scotch words, which no one here except my aunt can understand, but as to slurring my *r*'s and softening my *a*'s, and 'nabbing high English', I cannot—not even to please Aunt Bennet. I should only make a fool of myself, which she would be the first person to see, for she is what father used to call nimble-witted. I could not if I would hide that I am a Scotch girl; and I shall never wish to hide it. What! conceal that I am a countrywoman of St Margaret, and Queen Mary (poor woman!), and John Knox, and Sir Walter Scott, and Burns? Never! What would everybody in Inverlochan think if they heard such a proposal?"

Later on, when she "comes out" and finds how much she enjoys gaiety, pretty frocks and compliments, Flora makes "conscientious instinctive use of the props and stays within her reach in order not to grow what she called 'silly'—properly speaking, vain and frivolous. She was not going to lose sight either of her birthright or her identity."

Serial stories with a child heroine are rare among those appearing in the Victorian *G.O.P.*, but one such is *About Peggy Saville* (1898) by Jessie Mansergh, better known as Mrs G. de Horne Vaizey. I read this book myself as a child, over forty years after it was serialised, and I suppose it is among the best-known of the serials. Perhaps Peggy can hardly be called a child at fourteen, but she is certainly not yet a young lady, and she has an unsentimental comradeship with the boy characters in the story reminiscent of that enjoyed by Jo March and Laurie in Louisa M. Alcott's *Little Women*. *About Peggy Saville* was followed by *More About Peggy* in 1899.

Working-class heroines are in the minority in *G.O.P.* fiction, but they do appear from time to time. Ruth Lamb was an author who frequently championed the cause of the working girl. Her serial *Sackcloth and Ashes* (1892) deals very interestingly with work—the brutal, grinding work of really poor women. When the heroine first appears, though she is young and good-looking, she is so filthy that people draw away from her. A man with whom she talks on a tram gives her a small parcel which proves to be a cake of soap. Susannah decides she has been known for too long as "Smutty Sue" and puts the soap to good use. As the story unfolds,

Far right: the handsome and outspoken Miss Lawton, an American girl of spirit, is more than a match for the languid English Lord Beechcroft. In his loose-cut tweed suit, whose knickerbockers allow "the muscular perfection of his figure to be seen to advantage", he is said to be "as fine a type of masculine beauty as she of feminine".

THE GIRL'S OWN PAPER

Vol. XIV.—No. 667.]   OCTOBER 8, 1892.   [Price One Penny.

THE LITTLE GIRL IN GREY.

A STORY OF TWO CONTINENTS.

By HORACE TOWNSEND.

"'AH, BUT YOU'RE A LORD, AND THAT MAKES A DIFFERENCE—WITH MY PAPA.'"

ANSWERS TO CORRESPONDENTS.

MISCELLANEOUS.

Canariensis and Others.—1. Paddle away as much as you like, it is wonderfully strengthening to the feet and ankles. 2. We are almost afraid to offer any advice as to the length of time which girls ought to pass in the water. We have frequently offered our advice at the seaside, and it has invariably been rejected. Our private opinion is that twenty minutes will make a very fair average, but much depends on the constitution of the bather. When a bather of either sex finds that the finger tips become white instead of pink, it is a sign that the bath has been too long. Giddiness on coming out of the water tells the same story.

Maidenhair.—Girls of thirteen require at least eight hours' sound sleep, exclusive of the time occupied in the toilet before and after sleep; but they should manage it by going to bed early and not sitting up late.

Beryl Orsmond.—1. Make the diet of your cockatoo as simple as possible. Perhaps you have been allowing her to nibble at bones or to eat animal food. Give her a bath by all means, but don't put her in it yourself. If she needs a bath, instinct will teach her to use it. 2. You do not mention your age, so we cannot tell how much character your writing ought to have; it certainly is not too small, and it is perfectly legible, but it has a sort of character of its own, the lines slanting downwards instead of upwards, as is the usual feminine fashion. Practise writing with black-lined paper, and you will soon find yourself falling into the right way.

Zulu Hat.—1. Of course you do not "make both ends meet of your income" if on £300 per annum you "keep three servants." One is all you ought to keep, and you should undertake all the light part of the household work yourself. 2. Wreaths of grapes and a few poppies serve best as trimming for a Zulu hat.

Studenta.—Go on, enquiring spirit, with your methodical reading; it is one of the secrets of progress. We understand the quotation to refer to certain inferences erroneously drawn from observations made on the brain of the frog as the seat of sensation and mental action. Theology is not likely to be so easily overthrown.

Archimedes.—1. There is no way of pressing flowers so as perfectly to preserve their natural colour. The colour always fades more or less. But there is a method of drying them with sand and exposure to heat by which they retain their brilliancy pretty well, and also their original form. By this method they will remain in good preservation for several years. 2. The way to overcome the dislike of being alone is to make excellent company of yourself. Improve your mind, then, by reading and thought. Your handwriting might be better, and it will be, Archimedes, if you practice.

Alphonsia.—1. Your handwriting is very good for your age. But don't be satisfied; make it still better. 2. Who is afraid? why, bring common-sense to bear upon it. You should live where we do, and go upstairs at midnight to hear the owls hooting in the wood. Whenever you feel particularly nervous repeat to yourself the 4th verse of the 23rd Psalm; it is a fine cordial for all timid folks.

Julia.—For potato cakes take ten ounces floury potatoes, boiled and smoothly pounded. When just warm add gradually a little salt, six ounces of flour, and three ounces of butter; no liquid is required. When the ingredients are thoroughly mixed, roll the dough into thin cakes the size of a captain's biscuit. Bake in a moderate oven or on a girdle; when done, split open, butter well, and serve very hot.

A Young Mother.—1. We are glad that the article on washing has proved so useful to you. In the second and third chapters you will probably find the further information you require. When ironing such small articles as you mention, the oval-shaped or "egg-iron" will do you good service. 2. We regret that we cannot tell you how to eradicate stains made by Condy's Fluid. An eminent chemist informs us that a long and persistent course of bleaching with chlorine might, at length, wear out the stains, but thinks the fabric itself would be worn-out or made tender during the operation. We thank you heartily for your kind and appreciative letter.

An Unsophisticated Child of Nature.—Kindly choose a shorter *nom de plume* when next you write. Do not be uneasy about your tortoise. The little gentleman has very likely got a will of his own. Try him with cabbage or greens, but he will go off to sleep by and bye, and when summer days come, he will most assuredly make up for his long fast.

Blanche.—1. At your age you need not be alarmed at your hair getting thin; it is probable that your system is a little out of order. Attend to your health; eat and drink nothing that stimulates or heats the system; take a teaspoonful or two of cream of tartar now and then of a morning. Use a hard brush for five minutes every day, morn and night, and the following stimulating pomade. Go to a respectable chemist and tell him to mix you two drachms of Wilson's stimulating ointment in an ounce and a half of nicely-scented pomade. Rub a little of this well into the roots of the hair every day, and wash once a week with juniper-tar soap, or mild carbolic acid soap. 2. Take the cold bath all winter if you are *certain* you feel the benefit of it. If you have any doubts, take a *little* of the chill off.

Sybil.—Every evening take a note-book and make a list of things to be done on each successive day, a certain time of the day being allotted to each task—some book to be read, some needlework to be continued or completed, household arrangements, or setting in order of drawers, or rooms to be done, letters too long neglected to be written, visits to be paid, or shopping, errands, and work for others it not for yourself. "Whatsoever thy hand findeth to do, do it with thy might." Life is too important and too brief for the indulgence of indolence. You write fairly well.

Margarita Avenal.—The lines you quote do not appear to be from the pen of any well-known author. They are not poetry. Thank you for your nice letter.

Wallflower.—The lady has the privilege of recognising a gentleman or not, at her own discretion. Your grammar and spelling should be better learnt before you attempt to write letters, and you have employed six capital letters in the wrong places within a space of eight lines.

S. W., H. H., and H. L. write a very fine free hand. That of H. H.'s is good, but less so than S. W.'s. That of H. L.'s is scarcely yet formed, but might prove very good with care.

"ALL SOLD, MISS. WOULD YOU LIKE TO ORDER THE JANUARY PART IN GOOD TIME?"

A Scotchwoman spoils her hand by sloping it the wrong way.

Jarvis Street.—We regret to tell you that our editorial staff is complete; and we already have close connections with Canada.

Helena.—Much of the Litany used in the Church of England is of very ancient Christian origin, but Cranmer made some part of it. Your hand is a particularly good one.

H. S.—P. P. C. means *Pour prendre congé*; P. D. A. *Pour dire adieux*. See our articles on the subject of writing.

Madeline and Imagination.—The proper pronunciation of the name Cabul is "Caw-bull," the emphasis laid on the first syllable. Your writing is insignificantly small. "Imagination" writes very well.

Mab.—The cause of the death of your "table-plants" may probably be traced to lighting your room with gas. You appear to write with a badly-cut quill pen, so we can scarcely judge of your writing.

Courtenay.—The pillows of a bed should be covered in the day-time with the quilt, and if the bed be an old-fashioned four-poster, the curtains at the head of the bed should be folded and laid across them, with the ends meeting in the middle. It is more usual to trim the pillows with frillings or lace than the top sheet, but of course it looks pretty to have it so finished.

Moss Rose.—Our answers are made to correspondents so many in number that they have to wait for them. Ivy, like most climbing plants, renders the wall on which it grows more or less damp. It also injures the masonry, although it may for some time hold a ruin together.

Betty.—Doves eat hempseed, crumbs of bread, and indeed any grain almost. Your handwriting is good, but rather large.

Muggins.—If moths be already in a mattress, the latter will have to be taken to pieces, and properly baked by a man whose business it is. 2. The name Hugh should be pronounced as if written "Hu," the last two letters being mute. Handwriting not bad, but too large.

Junetta.—When the canary's claws have grown so long as to curl round the perch and endanger the catching of his feet in the bars of the cage they should be cut a little with very sharp strong scissors. You write a pretty hand.

Ruby.—You write with too hard a pen. Trim your dress with velveteen. See "Dress of the Month."

Dignitas.—You write a very good hand. We thank you for your kind and well expressed letter, and are glad that our correspondence columns interest you so much.

A. C. D.—1. You will find the tales of MM. Erckmann-Chartrain delightfully interesting. 2. The address of the Ladies' British Sanitary Association is 22, Berners-street, W. See Miss Rose Adams.

Anna.—We could not help you in this matter, as we wholly disapprove of Planchette and all kindred amusements.

Puck.—Chamois leather gloves are washed in a tepid lather.

Lilian Mary Graham.—Both your friends failed in good breeding. The gentleman should have taken the penny to pay for the stamp, as he had already laid the lady under an obligation by his prompt kindness in offering it to her. But allowing that the gentleman failed in good breeding, that is no excuse for the lady's declining the stamp altogether. Finding she was not allowed to pay for it, she should have accepted it with a graceful expression of thanks for the gift. Of the two, the lady's fault was the greater.

Cuckoo Flower.—*Vive la bagatelle* means "Success to trifling." Not a good sentiment, except interpreted that a little recreation is good for health of mind and body.

F. E. T. R.—Thank you very much indeed for your kind letter. We should strongly advise you not to work up for the examination, as it would most probably ruin what little health you have; and it is so obligatory on all of us to take care of our health. May God bless you, and strengthen you to carry out your resolutions. Your handwriting is beautiful, but the composition of your letter is marred by writing, "I think that *one* must examine *themselves* well."

A Scotch Girl suggests that every girl who has a friend's welfare at heart should *give* her a copy of The Girl's Own Paper, and she is kind enough to speak in unqualified terms of its value. She also says that she has introduced the Magazine to eight of her female friends, who are now subscribers. 1. This good little Scotch girl is informed that she can get the Index to vol. i., for one penny, or the Frontispieces to the monthly parts and Index for ninepence, and the beautiful cloth case for two shillings. This cloth case is to be had in many colours, but the editor, in strict confidence and in return for her nice letter, advises her to order the slate colour. Her bookbinder will put the book together at very little cost. 2. Stop plucking the hair from your chin. All will come right in time. Your writing is unequal, part of the letter is written well, and the other part indifferently.

Flossie.—Your writing is not formed yet, but you do your best and are very careful. When you have had a little more practice, your writing will be more easily performed and will look pleasanter. We cannot possibly remember why we did not answer your previous letters.

Emmeline Marie Laurence.—Sing "Darby and Joan" at your grandparents' golden wedding. Nothing could be better for the purpose. It is simple, beautiful, and in several keys. "Always the same to your old wife Joan!" Would it not be splendid if every wife could say this of her husband.

H. M. E.—1. You should not do your lessons on Sundays. Read with earnest prayer your Bible and other good books between the hours of divine service, and maybe that the peace of God of which you speak might be imparted to you. Acknowledge your own unworthiness and sin, and implore God to receive you by virtue of His Son's merits. 2. Your writing is not good.

Millie E. T.—Wear a white cap and white cashmere dress. The plainer the better. Think more of your heart than your garment, and put the other questions to your parson.

Clarinda.—1. We do not know—and do not wish to know—who wrote the morbid lines which you quote. We think you had better consult a doctor, for you are evidently in a very bad state. 2. Your writing is scandalous.

Hazeldyne.—Why do you say that you do not care for music, and yet acknowledge that you play Bach, Beethoven, Haydn, and Mozart. Your sister says that you play well and have a very good touch. We counsel you not to be silly, for you are getting out of the dry-bones part of learning, and will be thankful, when you are older, that you are an accomplished pianist. Your writing is rather nice, and so is your sister's.

A Left-out One.—If it is true that you are selfish, lazy, bad tempered, plain, and unaccomplished, we do not wonder that nobody cares for you, and we trust that you will always keep at a respectful distance from us. Your portrait which you enclose, however, is that of a charming young damsel.

RUBY C.—Wash the crewel work in tepid water with soap, rinse it, and, if possible, wring through a machine, so as to make it perfectly dry.

ROMOLA.—You will find in the *Leisure Hour* for March an article on "Lamarck and Darwin," which will explain to you all about the doctrine of Evolution, showing how far it is true, with its relation to natural and revealed religion.

SPES.—Apply to the Admiralty, or if you live near a dockyard, make inquiries there.

CLAUDIA.—Use Pope's translation of the "Iliad" or the "Odyssey," if you cannot procure a more modern one. The "Conquest of Mexico," by Prescott, is an excellent book.

ONE OF ELEVEN.—There are Moravian schools at Fairfield, near Manchester, at Fulneek, near Leeds, and Pytherton, in Wiltshire. Address the Head Mistress in each case.

A SOLDIER'S FIANCÉE.—There is no other meaning than that the young lady has said "yes," and the young man is going away.

UNE GENEVOISE.—We were not at all "shock" at the style of your kind and funny little letter, and think your self-acquired knowledge of English wonderful. Order THE GIRL'S OWN PAPER from the Publisher, 56, Paternoster-row, E.C. The postage to Switzerland is 2d. each number.

SAILOR.—The belief that those who are born at sea belong to the parish of Stepney is included by Brand in his list of "Vulgar Errors."

QUERY.—There are no less than four martyrs, bishops, and saints called "Donatus," from any of whom the road may take its name.

A KENTISH GIRL.—Surnames were first used in England in the latter part of the tenth century. They were introduced by the Norman conquerors, and were chiefly derived from the names of the continental estates of the bearers of them, or from places within their seignories abroad. Camden says that "there is scarcely a single village in Normandy which has not surnamed a family in England." Families of native lineage also, after the example of the victors, adopted hereditary surnames, derived from manors and other localities. Amongst these we may reckon the De Fords, De Ashburnhams, and De Newtons.

AN INSTRUCTION SEEKER.—The names of the two thieves crucified with our Saviour are said, by tradition, to have been Dimas and Gestas, the former being he unto whom the promise was vouchsafed—"To-day shalt thou be with Me in Paradise." We believe it is supposed that the Hebrew words rendered "pieces of money," denoted a piece having on it the stamp or impression of a lamb or sheep, intimating thereby its current value. In Genesis xxxiii. 19, you will find it rendered "lambs" in the margin of your Bible. The "thirty pieces of silver" received by Judas was the "stater," a Greek silver coin, each worth about 2s. 1d., or perhaps more.

PET BIRDIE.—We have had a cat and a bird simultaneously, and watched the process of training, in reference to the former, performed daily by an old servant. She used to hold up the cat near the cage, and when it began to "chatter" at the bird she scolded and buffeted it with a handkerchief, then set it down on the floor, and drove it out of the room. The plan certainly succeeded, for whenever the cat saw the bird, after this discipline had been carried on for a certain time, it used to fly from the room as if chased by a pack of hounds. The servant was quite as fond of the cat as of the bird, and even preferred it of the two. But our bird remained in its cage; and if yours be free to fly about, its danger is far greater. We thank you for so kind a letter. Your writing is good.

CORAL.—Either the wax or the spirits of wine in which it was to be dissolved must have been of a very inferior kind, as we never knew the method to fail.

DOT and DANDY.—1. Pack the flowers in cotton-wool, very lightly, yet so as to cover them completely; and lay them in a cardboard box securely wrapped in paper. 2. A gentleman should give a lady whichever arm will permit her to take the inside of the footway or pavement. He should never place her on the outside.

JENNY JONES.—If you have no friends in town, yet have sufficient time for spending a few hours here, we advise your going direct to the British Museum or South Kensington, and make a study of one gallery after another. Then make a tour of the National and some of the other picture galleries, including Gustave Doré's, where you will find a comfortable place of rest when tired. We should advise you to go to these places provided with a

RULES

I. No charge is made for answering questions.

II. All correspondents to give initials or pseudonym.

III. The Editor reserves the right of declining to reply to any of the questions.

IV. No direct answers can be sent by the Editor through the post.

V. No more than two questions may be asked in one letter, which must be addressed to the Editor of THE GIRL'S OWN PAPER, *56, Paternoster-row, London, E.C.*

VI. No addresses of firms, tradesmen, or any other matter of the nature of an advertisement will be inserted.

cemetery, which was laid out by M. Brongniart, and first used on May 21, 1804.

A MOTHER OF A WORKING LAD.—Giddiness may arise from various causes. In your son's case we should say that it arose from weakness, and that tonics, wine, and a liberal diet would be beneficial. But we could not advise you as to what particular tonic he should take. You had better consult a medical man on the subject.

A READER OF THE GIRL'S OWN PAPER.—The different sounds of the letter "c" is one of the anomalies of the English alphabet. It is like "s" before "e," "i," and "y," as in "cell," "civil," "cymbal," except, "sceptic," "cymry;" hard like "k" before "a, o, u, r, l, t." The relative pronoun agrees with its antecedent in gender and number; in case it may be nominative, genitive, or objective, governed by a verb or a preposition. Example—"Who is that?" Answer, "The lady to whom you were introduced."

EDINBURGH.—If this young person be unable to discover a greater flaw in our magazine than an obvious oversight or misprint in reference to a single word, and that in a correspondence of such magnitude, we can only congratulate ourselves in having passed through the ordeal with rare success. We beg, at the same time, to offer her our sincere condolences on the pitiful disappointment which she must have experienced.

A CAMBRIDGE SENIOR.—1. We are not told how near the king permitted Gehazi to approach him; and without doubt he took care to keep him at a safe distance. Elisha and the servant whom he sent to speak with Naaman the leper did not catch the disease by speaking to him; nor did the "ten men that were lepers," who were healed by our Lord, communicate it by approaching Him or His disciples sufficiently near for speaking with Him. "Dwelling without the camp" was, of course, essential, as the disease was contagious; and it would not have been safe for others to enter their dwellings and touch anything which they had handled. 2. The illustration marked "a" shows a correct prism.

WALLFLOWER.—You had better try sand, glass, or emery paper, and use whichever of them answers best. Where the edges of the stone are sharp, be careful not to blunt them. "Genoa cake" is made as follows:—Ingredients required: Half a pound of flour, half a pound of butter, ditto sugar, four eggs, a small glass of brandy, and a little salt. Mix the flour, sugar, eggs, brandy and salt well together in a basin with a wooden spoon, then add the butter (merely melted by the side of the fire), and when this is thoroughly incorporated with the batter, pour it into an appropriately-sized tin baking - sheet (previously spread with

notebook, and thus impress on your memory all that you have seen. A visit now and then to the Crystal Palace would compensate you for your trouble, especially as there is an excellent reading-room and library there to which ladies have access on paying one penny. On certain days in the week the South Kensington is free; on others the charge for entrance is 6d. The British Museum and National Gallery are always free when open, but you must obtain information from the newspapers. 2. Your writing is almost too large already. The large modern hand is very coarse and vulgar.

SUSIE.—Jenny Lind (Madame Goldschmidt), is living. Gentlemen in England do not usually wear betrothal rings.

AN ÆSTHETIC SPARROW.—Père la Chaise was the favourite and confessor of Louis XIV., who made him the superior of a great establishment of the Jesuits on this spot, then named Mont Louis. The house and grounds were bought for a national

butter) to the thickness of about a quarter of an inch, and bake this in an oven moderately heated. When it is done, it should be turned out upon a sheet of paper, and cut, or stamped out, either in circular, oblong, oval, leaf-like, or any other fancy shape that taste may suggest. These may then be decorated with white of egg and sugar, prepared as for "méringues," or with icing prepared as directed for wedding-cakes.

G. E. C.—We think that, with a sheet of blotting paper and a hot iron, you might succeed in taking the grease spots out of the wall paper.

ERNEST'S WIFE.—Shrove Tuesday derives its name from the ancient practice, in the Church of Rome, of confessing sins and being shrived, or shrove, that is, obtaining absolution on this day. Pancakes were originally to be eaten after dinner, to stay the stomachs of those who went to be shriven. The Shrove bell was called the "Pancake bell," and the day of shriving "Pancake Tuesday."

There never was a greater mistake made than marrying to reform a man; nor should a woman perjure herself by taking such solemn vows and making such declarations as those in marriage, if she do not really love a man. You should not marry for pity's sake either, nor as a mark of gratitude for family favours rendered by him, nor think of uniting yourself to any man, however good, so long as you feel the smallest disinclination for such a change of condition. If, as his family say, your refusal will drive him back into evil habits, he is not a really reformed character, and is acting on no high principle, and therefore, by their own showing, is no safe husband for you.

TROUBLED ONE in 1891 "thinks of shutting the stable door when the horse is stolen", which sounds ominous. The reply continues:

Why did you allow this very excellent young man to kiss you on several occasions when alone? You should have objected on the first attempt; and said that you could not allow such familiarity except from an engaged lover. Be sure he does not respect you the more for permitting him to take such a liberty so often without resistance or rebuke. You have only yourself to blame.

OLIVE ... appears to be suffering from the society of too many young men. Do not allow any man to reach the point of proposing to you if you do not mean to accept him; and do not accept any man as an intended husband whom you do not love. You ought to be ashamed of loving any man who does not love you and desire to win your love. If you need advice on such points, consult your mother. [1888]

In the reply to A COUNTRY LASSIE in 1887, class is the problem, and the gulf of a century between our day and hers is never wider:

In reference to your partiality for a working man (he being a religious man), we think you would not only act in an unseemly way, but a most reprehensible way, to set aside the natural feelings of your father and your other relatives, by marrying a man in a lower position in life, however respectable in character. We are all placed in the respective stations in life which we occupy by our Heavenly Father's appointment. You will be spared much trial and suffering as a single woman, and you had better leave your future altogether in the Lord's hands.

NOBODY'S OWN is told in 1887:

You are very unwise to set your heart so much on changing your present condition. You seem to be blessed with a comfortable home, and as you are not obliged to earn your bread, you have the more time to devote to others. Try to study what will help and please the members of your own home circle, and to organise a little society amongst your young friends for helping the sick and sorrowful by your visits or handiwork. If your Divine Master should require you to undertake new responsibilities as a married woman, He will send you a suitable husband.

The reply to BELLADONNA, who was obviously considering profiting by the fact that 1884 was a Leap Year, is more brusque:

Are you out of your mind, or were you born with any brains? A man would make a bad choice if he accepted an offer of marriage from any girl; for one who could so far set aside all natural feelings of maidenly delicacy as to ask him to marry her, would be quite unfit to be the mistress of a house and to bring up daughters of her own. Are you so utterly incapable of understanding a joke as to imagine that the recurrence of an extra day in February could justify you in throwing off all reserve, and degrading yourself thus?

TO OUR CORRESPONDENTS.

OUR readers will, doubtless, have observed that more space than usual has lately been given to that department of our paper called "Answers to Correspondents." This has, of course arisen from an increase in the number of letters received from the girls since the commencement of the magazine.

It must not be supposed, however, that these extra answers represent replies to all questions sent to us, as some of our correspondents seem to suppose. Indeed we regret to say that it is far otherwise, for every morning we receive letters answers to which would occupy more than half a weekly number.

It is, therefore, certain that many letters must remain unanswered.

Now with a view to fewer disappointments in the future, the editor wishes to say that no girl should ask more than two questions in one letter, and these should be sensible questions, clearly and briefly stated.

From this date, therefore, any letters containing more than two questions will be destroyed unanswered.

The correspondents should select initials or short and uncommon pseudonyms, avoiding "A Constant Reader," "A Lover of the G. O. P.," and other such hackneyed phrases. They should also refrain from calling themselves by such flattering names as "Fair Maid of Perth," &c., and from giving themselves the names of men.

Many letters are sent to us from various parts asking one and the same question. In this case we give one answer only, leaving the others to receive the information from that.

Of course, many questions are put to us, which, from an insufficient knowledge of various facts, we are totally unable to answer. Other letters, again, are frivolous, and prove the writers to possess an undue anxiety as to their personal appearance, as, for instance, questions on the complexion, figure, colour of the hair, &c. Such questions will, for the future, remain unanswered, as being contrary to the aims and objects of the paper.

It is therefore needless for girls to send us locks of hair and photographs for criticism.

When our girls need information that would be of real service, relating to education, domestic economy, work, recreation, and other subjects, we shall consider it a privilege to supply it, if it be in our power; and we shall also be heartily thankful to continue to give our counsel and advice to any anxious and troubled soul needing it; for, did we not say at the outset that we should "aim at being a counsellor, playmate, guardian, instructor, companion, and friend, and that we should help to prepare our readers for the responsibilities of womanhood and for a heavenly home"?

Above: an editorial comment from August 7, 1880 (the pencil marking appears on the original issue).

Far left: a page of replies, April 1, 1882.

The answer to A SERVANT in 1886 strikes a regrettably tongue-in-cheek note:

Not having seen, and knowing nothing of your two suitors—the cab-driver who is lame, and the flute-player who is deaf—we could not decide between them. Do they bear equally good characters as honest, industrious, and sober men? Are both good-tempered, healthy, good-looking, and equally well-to-do? Have both got a nice little home to take you to? And has either of them got a mother-in-law waiting for you, and keeping a house there already? Lastly, which cares for you the most, and have you no fancy for one more than the other?

PERPLEXED is answered in the following year:

Without being a teetotaller, we feel with you in reference to the odious practice of drinking a gin cocktail every morning before lunch. The probability is that drunkenness will, sooner or later, be the result. No wonder he is cross when you expostulate with him; the drinking of spirits has that tendency; it spoils both temper and digestion. Besides this, it is an exceedingly low, vulgar habit. Such a beginning on his part gives no promise of happiness on a wife's.

A hundred years has not altered the problem of the teenager who wants to go out with boys before her parents think she should. E.G.H. is rapped over the knuckles in 1892:

A young girl of sixteen and some months is very far too young to be in search of "lovers". Your aunt is quite right in not allowing you to "go out in the evening", especially if "very handsome", as you say you are. It is a disgrace to the mothers of "some of your girl friends, not nearly as old as you" (they must be in short frocks and bibs), if they have had lovers for some time.

Even without the full text of the letter from E.G.H. the authentic note of disgruntled adolescence can be heard at a distance of more than eighty years.

A still more mordant reply is addressed to FIFTEEN in 1892:

Your letter is a disgrace to you. The way in which you speak of your mother's care and watchfulness over you is little to your credit. It is not "chronic inquisitiveness", it is a part of her duty. She has a right to know what you do, where you go, and whom you meet. We hope that any mother who has two daughters, one of seventeen and one of fifteen who read this paper, and who take walks in the country without a maid or a chaperon, will discover the danger incurred by her daughters in meeting and walking with strange men clandestinely. Have you no self-respect, any more than no dutiful feeling? The coarse slang you employ betrays the low order of men and boys with whom you associate.

FIFTEEN can hardly have been gratified by that reply, especially if her mother happened also to be a reader of the G.O.P. However, bracing, tonic admonitions are the rule in these pages:

ALTA.—It is wrong to persistently refuse to sing if you have a voice. Nothing is so thoroughly wretched to a stranger as to meet a girl at a musical party who refuses to exert herself to take part in the entertainment. It is conceited to be nervous. Nobody wants to hear you. It is the music of the composer and the words of the song that they wish you to expound to them. [1880]

Far right: miscellaneous replies, August 11, 1883.

154

Molly.—Your face will often become flushed if your feet are cold, but such troubles arise also from a weak digestion, or mental work too soon after eating.

Limy Boy.—The articles on "The Duties of Servants" will be found at pages 534, 646, vol. ii.

Impatience.—The 15th October, 1865, was a Sunday.

Pansy.—We do not know of any Institute to which old kid gloves are of value.

Ging'oring and Blindbat.—A cardinal of the Roman Church is addressed as "Your Eminence;" the Pope, as "Your Holiness," and "Holy Father."

Edith.—You must either advertise or obtain the situation by inquiring amongst your friends. Fancy-work is of little value at present, as nearly everyone does it for themselves.

E. G. B.—Wash the white feathers with curd-soap and warm water, shake dry before a fire, and then curl each filament with a blunt pen-knife, or a paper-knife.

Pussy S. E. A.—We must refer you to page 751, vol. iii. for the meaning of the use of the letters "M." and "N." in the Catechism. The pronunciation of the name of the French town "Cannes" is like that of the English word "Can." Your writing is so illegible, we can scarcely read it. See "Tortoises," page 367, vol. iii.

Queen Esther.—The allusion to "Vanda" is from "The Betrothed," by Sir Walter Scott. She was the spirit with the red hand, who appeared in the haunted chamber to the heroine of the story. Egbert was the first king of all England. He ascended the throne A.D. 827, and was the first of the line of Saxon kings which ended with the Norman conquest.

Useless One.—1. Several queries on the same subject were answered at page 496, vol. iv. (the number for May 5, 1883). It is not a text in the Bible. 2. Write to the secretary of the East London Hospital for Children, or to that in Great Ormond-street, and make inquiries direct.

Lucini Marcello.—Cut the bread-and-butter very thinly, take off the crust and roll it. There are several heads under which the various styles of musical compositions are classified, amongst which are the classical, operatic, martial, dance, and sacred music, besides others.

Mayflower.—Change the blotting-paper in which you press the flowers frequently. This question has been often answered.

L. E. S.—A gentleman would take off his glove, not a lady in that case.

Bookkeeper.—The tale of Robinson Crusoe, written by De Foe, was founded on the adventures of Alexander Selkirk, but the hero himself and his man Friday were the creations of De Foe. But we do not enjoy the story less because of its not being wholly fact, and you must accept the amusement and instruction of "Robina Crusoe" in the same way.

Querksy.—We do not approve of such foolish attempts to alter the appearance, and must decline to answer you.

Rosa Bonheur.—Ladies as a rule do not fee male servants. When staying at a friend's house, therefore, you would fee the upper housemaid; in a smaller house you would fee the parlourmaid and housemaid. Where there is a butler or a man out of livery, you would fee him if he attended to your errands or letters.

The Artless Thing.—Cards are not now sent out after a wedding, and cake only to relations or *very* intimate friends. When the bride receives her friends, some wedding-cake may be offered with the afternoon tea. We could not say; it would depend on the position of the bridegroom.

Elsie Caird complains, like many other English girls, of having had her digestive organs completely put out of order, and to a very serious extent indeed, by a three years' residence in Germany (probably at school), where the cookery was exceedingly greasy in character. The only safe plan to adopt is to procure the advice of a good doctor, and carefully follow the course of treatment he may recommend. Medicine for the liver will be necessary, and possibly a liver tonic. A diet consisting of little if any meat for a time, and neither butter nor one atom of fat of any kind, nor of fried food. A little boiled fish or roast or boiled fowl, and light puddings, a little dressed vegetables, stewed or roast apples, but no oranges. Avoid study or any employment for an hour after dinner, and half an hour after other meals. Dine early, masticate slowly and thoroughly. If the sickness take place after eating, try a dessertspoonful of chicken broth, hot or cold, at a time, and swallow a small scrap of ice immediately after it, and remain perfectly still. This may stop the sickness and restore strength to the stomach, to enable it to do more very shortly. This is all we dare advise. See a doctor, for your case appears to be serious. One visit would at least suffice to supply you with a suitable prescription for medicine.

Old Duke.—"All rights reserved," means that the book or magazine and its contents cannot be translated nor used in any way for re-publication without permission of the publishers or author.

obliged to come to London, and, like anyone else, walk about your favourite localities and search for what you want.

Griselda.—We fear our business engagements would not permit of our undertaking any extra work.

Ignoramus.—If the lady be at home when you call, and not her husband, leave your husband's card for him.

May.—Write and congratulate the bridegroom, and express the hope of making the bride's acquaintance at some future day.

Carina.—Mustard and cress may be grown in a sponge. Reading aloud slowly and distinctly will probably be of service to you.

Nan, Nan.—Inquire at any chemist's for the prepared charcoal, which is sold in bottles, as well as in biscuit form. Full directions are given with each bottle, and there are, we believe, several sizes and prices.

Jo (Bristol).—There is no preventive for mosquitoes that we know of, save the "smudges," or little fires, used in America, and lit in the evening all round the houses in the Bush, so that the smoke may drive the mosquitoes away. Net blinds are also useful in the windows, and net or muslin curtains closely-fitting over the beds.

Sunbeam.—There is nothing to prevent your adding the "de" before your name, if you consider you are entitled to it, and there is no one to pay for doing so.

THE SUMMER NUMBER.

Mother (restraining her tears).—"We must bear up, my darling, and must try to borrow it from a friend. Oh, why did we neglect to order it in time!"

The "Heralds' College," Queen Victoria-street, London, E.C., would be the place to which you should apply for information on the subject. They have every information relating to English families of any note. What is called an "Heraldic Stationer, we believe, would also tell you; there are many advertising in London papers.

Nellie Burke.—We think that the lines lack originality, so much so that we have been trying to remember the hymn from which they are taken, probably unconsciously even to yourself.

"Grandmother Dear."—One of the great drawbacks to German schools for English girls is the diet, which seems in many cases to have affected the digestion and the health of those sent to them. Growing girls need careful treatment, and this subject should be well considered.

Alice Everton.—We are gratified by your letter, which is well expressed, and fairly well written. In reference to "washing and starching a black print dress," see pages 18, 107, and 219, vol. ii., under "How to Wash and Iron."

Winifred.—We regret to say that your verses are not "poetry." The versification is quite incorrect, and no poetical and original ideas occur in them. Your handwriting promises well, but is not yet quite formed

one if only sloped the right way, like "Mater's," which is a good one. "Maude" writes like her mother, or at least much in the same style. "Lillian" gives good promise, but her letters are upright.

Speranza and Patienza.—The poems enclosed, "Why?" and "Infelix," we shall have pleasure in inserting in The Girl's Own Paper (in "The Girl's Own Page"), if you send us a certificate of their being your own, a matter of rule, not personal to yourself; and at the same time state your age. We admire your poems much. Yes, we number many of your countrywomen amongst our correspondents. Your sister might use some wash for her hair unmixed with any oil or grease. It ought to shine; rough black hair would be frightful.

Lilian C.—A person with a "white" skin and "blue eyes" could not be termed a "brunette." To be thus described, the skin should either be of a clear olive hue, like a southron, or of a nut-brown complexion, like a gipsy, and the red colour should be like that of a russet-apple. Reduce the size of your writing and slope the letters the right way, and you will write a beautiful hand.

Ada and Lizzie.—Your quotation—

"Oh, woman! in our hours of ease,
Uncertain, coy, and hard to please,"

is from Sir Walter Scott's poem, "The Lady of the Lake." The term "blue-stocking" originated in a learned society formed at Venice in the year 1400, the members, men and women, adopting as a distinguishing mark the wearing of blue stockings. On dying out there, it appeared in Paris in 1590, the lady *savantes* taking up the idea warmly. It came to England in 1780, and was patronised by Mrs. Montague, and died out in 1840 in the person of the last member of the society, Miss Monckton, afterwards Countess of Cork.

A. A.—We consider your little poem ("Sowing and Reaping") superior to the majority which we receive for review. May you hereafter realise the full happiness of the glorious "reaping" time to which you refer.

F. C. C. and P.—A full description of Her Majesty's household is to be found at pages 21 and 154, vol. ii. The duties of the various officers are there named in detail.

Floss.—To make a decoction of sarsaparilla, digest two and a half ounces for half an hour of the cut Jamaica sarsaparilla in one and a half pints of boiling water; then boil for ten minutes and strain. The dose is from a wine-glassful to half a pint.

Carrie Leach.—In reference to the salt mines of Wieliczka, Poland, it is true that there are halls and passages, a chapel containing statues cut out of salt; the mine is perfectly dry and airy, and the miners are a fine race of men, and their labour is healthy. But it is not true that any of them live underground, for they rarely remain below the surface for more than eight hours daily. How well you write for eight years old, and you express yourself very well!

Penhurst writes to tell us that an English girl at Amalfi has suggested that, as the inscription on the monumental slab covering the grave of Queen Katharine of Aragon, in Peterborough Cathedral, is obliterated, all girls spelling their Christian name in the same way should subscribe for putting up a brass there to her memory. She has sent the first donation herself, and others have followed her example. The idea appears to be a popular one, and Mrs. Perowne will receive any further subscriptions sent to the Deanery, Peterborough. 2. "A man of Kent" signified one born east of the Medway. These men went out with green boughs to William the Conqueror, and in return had all their ancient privileges confirmed to them. They call themselves "the *invicti*." A "Kentish man" is only a resident of that county, without reference to his birthplace.

Shamrock.—We acknowledge your kind letter with thanks, and regret that the verses you have sent us are not suitable for insertion in our paper. They only consist of prose in rhyme.

Alice.—We are very glad to hear that you and your friends have succeeded in saving from £9 to £12 a year through the judicious instructions on the subject of dress supplied by a "Lady Dressmaker." The names "Alice" and "Alicia" count for one and the same.

S. E. C.—If you have failed in removing the machine-oil from your carpet by means of heat and blotting-paper, by benzine, and by washing with soap, we think you had better send it to a cleaner; or else, if practicable, you had better have the nearest seam ripped, and turn the outside edges of the carpet to the middle, so placing the stain at the wall, where less noticeable, and where a chair may cover it. The table will require to be repolished.

Daisy.—We should never recommend anything of the kind. We think that plenty of soap and water, daily exercise, and wholesome food are much better.

VIXEN.—In painting on satin, you should mix a little white of egg with the colour, together with Chinese white; this will supply a good glaze, and also prepare the surface of the material. We shall give an article on the subject. Another mode of preparation is to size the satin, by brushing it over with a decoction made of a pinch of alum and another of isinglass, dissolved in a tumbler of hot water. Then leave it to dry. The Chinese white will be found to adhere longer by mixing it with a small quantity of water-colour megilp.

MAY.—We thank you for the present of your pretty specimen card. There is such a "glut" of them at present in the market, that you will have to dispose of them, if you can, at stationers' shops in your own neighbourhood, or through friends elsewhere.

Above: answers to readers' queries on art, June 26, 1880.

Far right: elegantly decorated, a page of replies from August 7, 1886.

KATE WREN.—You might as well "cry for the moon" in your position as a domestic servant. If eligible for a different calling, enabling you to have a home of your own, you might have a piano and practise if you liked. [1891]

VIOLET seems to be very young and foolish. She drinks vinegar, and writes love poems, and does not seem to have grasped the purpose of her life here, which is to serve and love God and her brother, and come short in none of her daily home duties. To take much vinegar means to destroy her digestion and deteriorate the blood, and she will cease to be a worthy object of love if she fall into ill-health through her own folly. [1889]

A DAUGHTER OF CANADA (aged 13) must be crazy, and had far better attend to her lessons than worry herself and us with such perpetually-repeated and unprofitable enquiries. [1886]

POPPY.—From the constant repetitions of questions we think our girls must, many of them, have heads like sieves. See our articles* on "How to converse agreeably", "Good breeding in daily converse". We have done all we could to educate our girls in these matters, and cannot continue to repeat ourselves.

One wonders whether the criticism of handwriting which appears so regularly was solicited:

B.R. (Ardmore House).—Your troubles arise from a lowered state of the general health. Consult a doctor as to your home and its healthiness, diet, and exercise. Your handwriting is shocking, and the tone of your letter foolish and flippant. [1884]

AN ONLY GIRL.—We think your writing quite the most ugly we have ever seen. [1890]

Occasionally there is a dig at a reader's use of English:

MURIEL says their house "is *infected* with ants!" Had they measles, or whooping-cough, or what? Perhaps you mean that the house was *infested* with them. [1891]

One really unkind reply is addressed to SUBSCRIBER in 1892:

Oil your head and hair thickly until entirely free. We are surprised that you should ask so disgusting a question to be answered in print in a refined paper! Go to some nurse, and do not write to us again until thoroughly clean.

Probably B.R. deserved to be rebuked for her folly and flippancy, but poor SUBSCRIBER! Poor ANNIE GRAHAM, too, who is told "One of your questions respecting medical treatment is scarcely a delicate one, and we decline to answer it."

Undeterred, readers continued to write trustfully on an enormous variety of subjects. They frequently sent their poems for criticism, which was rarely enthusiastic. The reply to THEODORA is a fair example: "The enclosed poetry is harmless. We are sure it amused you to write it." So

* An extract from one of the "Good breeding" articles to which the Editor refers gives something of their flavour: "It would be kind and judicious in your converse with some old gentleman to draw him out on the subject of his travels, adventures, military or naval service, and exploits of bygone years, and the interest you showed, in words ever so few, could prove quite a refreshment to him." (1883)

ANSWERS TO CORRESPONDENTS

ATHELIS must find a standard of wrong and right in reading for herself, or she will always be miserable. If on rising from the perusal of any book she feels a better girl, more wishful to act rightly, and more conscientious in judging her actions, the book has done her good. During her girlhood it is well to be strict in everything she reads, as her mind is unformed, and amusing reading means, not rest and recreation, but generally mental dissipation.

THISTLE must read the various articles by "Medicus" on the hair, and be guided by them in her treatment of it. A good cleansing and softening wash for the head is composed of camphor and borax—of each one ounce in a quart of boiling water. Keep in a bottle, and when needed apply a little with a sponge, rubbing well in.

HOMESPUN.—Your letter, so well expressed and kindly, too, was read with interest. It did you credit, and were the writing a little smaller it would be better. We regret that your former letter was not answered, and we do not now recall the question it contained. Accept our best wishes.

LOTINCHA.—Carisbrooke Castle was once a British and Roman fortress. Cerdic, founder of the kingdom of the West Saxons, took it in 530. William Fitz-Osborne, Earl of Hereford (temp. William I.), gave it its Norman character. The imprisonment of Charles I. within it took place between November, 1647, and November, 1648; and the death of his daughter, the Princess Elizabeth, on September 8th, 1650, history states, of a broken heart, at the early age of fifteen. Your writing is very legible, but lacks grace.

AN AUSTRALIAN.—We could not venture to offer you an opinion as to Florida, especially as a residence for delicate people. You had better procure and study one or more books on the subject of the climate and the best locality, away from the swamps—"Down South," by Lady Duffus Hardy, and Barber's "Florida for Tourists and Settlers."

BLANCHE JANE (Canada).—This is the last notice that we shall take of your silly letters. Learn your lessons, read your Bible, and make and mend your own clothes, and waste no more time in writing such rubbish.

E. GRAY.—The sect of the Manichæans was founded by a native of Persia, who was born about the year A.D. 250. It was a fusion of Zoroastrianism and gnostic Christianity. Amongst other heretical dogmas, he maintained that the human body of Christ was a mere phantom, and His sufferings only apparent. As for Manichæus himself, he claimed to be the Blessed Paraclete promised by Christ.

FORGET-ME-NOT.—You should study our series of articles on good breeding and etiquette, under all circumstances and in every position of society. You should not bow perpetually on meeting and re-meeting an acquaintance. You can look into a shop or speak to your companion so as not to catch his eyes; but should you do so, give a smile with the slightest inclination of the head. Sometimes the Lord sees fit to permit you to be tried by temptations, and it is His will that we should look to Him for help, and grace, and strength to "fight the good fight of faith."

ENGLISH GIRL.—Pennies bearing the date 1864 have never been "called in," nor do we know where the foolish story of "the bar of gold that was dropped into the metal from which they were cast" originated; but they are of no more value than other pennies, and only one shilling can be got for twelve.

PETER CAMERON had better wear gloves, with the tips of the fingers soaked in alum-water, when she is reading, to prevent her biting her nails. A princess dress is the simplest dress to make for a doll.

I PENSIERI NON PAGANO GABELLE.—We cannot imagine how you came to think claret could be a teetotal drink, at any time. It is a wine, just as much as Burgundy or champagne.

UGLY MUG.—As a rule, it is both polite and more considerate to repay borrowed stamps with stamps, for though you give the penny at the time, it does not repay the trouble of buying another stamp and fetching it from the post-office. With elderly people this point of view should always be considered in borrowing them.

MAUD.—We must refer you to our indexes in reference to the complexion. Probably your diet is unsuitable, or you eat too fast, or you need internal rather than external remedies.

VIRTUOUS INDIGNATION does not know what she is talking about. Where does it say that godparents are "responsible for our sins until we are confirmed"? You invent a difficulty for yourself, and then profess yourself virtuously indignant. The duties of sponsors are to see that the child be religiously instructed and shall enjoy certain religious privileges in course of time. Remember this, that, quite apart from any promise or engagement made for him, his obligations to his Maker and Redeemer are as great and binding by every law of duty and gratitude, whether such promises are made or not. As yet you only scribble, and you should write copies daily to form your hand.

PETERHOFF.—We have heard it said that "no dead donkey is ever seen anywhere," not that they never die. Many complete disappearances are always taking place. Where do all the pins go? We think the former go to the knackers. See answer to "E. Gray" respecting your second query.

H. Y. Z.—The serviette is not refolded by the guest, but left generally on the chair on which he or she sits. At home asparagus may be eaten held in the fingers, but at a more formal repast the tops are cut off on the plate and eaten with the fork, like any other vegetable.

F. A. C.—We are obliged by your letter giving the address of the Midland Reading Society—secretary, Miss Cowper, Hillesden, Buckinghamshire, which gives prizes in money and sends its rules gratis.

BEULAH TERRACE.—We can only advise you to get the "Handy Guide to Emigration," by Mr. Paton, published by Stock, 379, Oxford-street, W. In that every one of the colonies is mentioned and every information given; price 6d. only.

L. T. G. (New Zealand).—Certainly, our paper patterns are sent to the colonies, including your own. You have only to send an order for what you require and a post-office order for the money due for the patterns. Your handwriting is not yet formed. Any set of copperplate copies would suit you in small round-hand.

TROUBLED ONE.—We are told in the Scriptures that "the Gospel shall be preached to all nations," not that it will be received, nor that the conversion of all nations will be the result: far otherwise, for our Lord says, "When the Son of Man cometh shall He find faith on the earth?"—at so low an ebb will it be found; and even "the love of many shall wax cold." We cannot tell when "the end will be." We must watch.

AFFLICTED HARRIET had better leave off eating late suppers, and avoid going to sleep or lying on her back in bed. She probably breathes through her mouth by day instead of her nose—a bad habit, which she must check. It would be well for her if she did read "Luke and Belinda" under the circumstances.

HEN.—We do not think the curse in question would be a good possession, and we certainly should not give any information where to get it. Why do you want it?

KISMET.—The evil actions which you name, such as petty pilferings, and other sins, should not hinder your making a solemn and sincere preparation for presenting yourself at the Lord's table. If you have quarrelled with anyone, make it up so far as, on your own side, you can do so. If you have stolen, restore what you have taken. If you have neglected your daily prayers, resume them; and, having humbly confessed to God your utter unworthiness, and prayed for His pardon and grace, present yourself at the holy table in the spirit of that beautiful hymn—

"Just as I am, without one plea,
But that Thy blood was shed for me,
And that Thou bid'st me come to Thee,
O, Lamb of God I come!"

Certainly, you must tell your stepmother the truth about the birdcage, and clear the boy's character before you presume to partake of the Lord's Supper.

ONE IN TROUBLE.—Your question is one more for a good surgeon than for us; but we do not think that, having had one operation, you had better try another without the best possible advice.

STEPHANOTIS.—Read "Lissom Hands and Pretty Feet," page 348, vol. i. You could not have the swellings on your joints "taken out." You might as well propose that when your nose is swelled from a bad cold and becomes inflamed that it should be "taken out" likewise. Wear straight, square-toed shoes, with low broad heels and broad soles.

IVY must read the articles of "Medicus." Her question is so vague that she must only try the measures recommended by him, which are safe and reliable.

MAUDE JAMES must consult a doctor, and be guided by him as to diet and regimen.

J. WHITE.—Your quotation is taken from Campbell's "Pleasures of Hope"—

"What though my winged hours of bliss have been
Like angel visits—few and far between."

LADY CLARICE.—We should think you had better ask him not to smoke at all, if you have any influence with him under the circumstances.

EVERYTHING AND SOMEBODY.—We should think there is something wrong in your mode of living, and can only advise you to read the advice of "Medicus."

TROUBLED ONE should consult a doctor about her general health.

EDUCATIONAL.

LESLIE and ANNIE FRY.—1. We have not got our series of articles on "Good Breeding" and the "Rules of Etiquette" in separate form. In the *Girl's Own Indoor Book* and the *Outdoor Book* you will find four of the series. Others amongst them are in vol. ii., pp. 73 and 314; in vol. iii., pp. 90, 163, 278, and 419; in vol. iv., pp. 74 and 403; in vol. v., pp. 38, 98, 262, 363, and 474. We have not space to enumerate more.—2. Almost any colour would suit "Leslie" from the description given of herself—dark ruby, or a full blue, depending on the season.

POLARIS.—Ladies are trained as teachers of the Kindergarten system of instruction at the Ladies' College of Cheltenham. The sister of the Head Master at Harrow, Miss Welldon, superintends and directs it. A house is provided for students. The entire expense of board and teaching is about fifty guineas a year. In London there are six training colleges and about twenty - seven schools. Also, there are training colleges for teachers at Bedford. Address Miss Sim, The Crescent; and at Manchester, Miss Snell, 94, Acomb Street, Greenheys.

MRS. E. B. ELLMAN.—We thank you for informing us of the resignation of your daughter from the secretaryship of so many branches of education united in her Girls' Club, and also for the address of the new Secretary who has undertaken to supply her place since her marriage, viz., Miss Davies, High Street, Coleford, Gloucestershire.

MISS J. K. MORTON.—You do not name your new club, but it seems to be of a literary character, admitting girls up to twenty years of age, and requiring a subscription of 6d. a year (too little, we think, to provide a half-yearly prize). Address Secretary, at Wilson House, Wilson Road, Birchfields, Birmingham.

F. VON H. AND S. R. N.—There are several Musical Practising Societies. Amongst them there is the Musical Association at Richmond House, Redland Green, Bristol; address Miss Mary Castle, the Secretary; and The Musical Society, Secretary, Miss McLandsborough, Lindan Terrace, Manningham, Bradford, Yorkshire.

MISS AMY FIRTH.—We are glad to have been the means of procuring members for your Practising Society, and give notice to our readers that your term commenced on November 1st; also, that when writing for your rules (to your address, Trinity House, Bradford), a stamp should invariably be sent. It is little creditable to the fifty girls writing for them to have omitted to enclose the amount due for postage, and of course it diminishes the amount which would otherwise have been allocated to prizes.

MISCELLANEOUS.

KITTY.—Nineteen is not too young to be engaged, but far too young to be married. And, indeed, we think that you will find occupation enough in the next three or four years in learning how to make a home happy and comfortable, and in improving your education, which seems to have been much neglected.

F. M.—"How to Study the English Bible?" A small book with this title, by the Rev. Canon Girdlestone, Principal of Wycliffe Hall, Oxford, will be very helpful to you. It is published at 5s., Paternoster Row.

A. B.—Yes; there is a small private Home of Rest for girls in business, Post Office clerks, school teachers, etc. Address, Miss H. Mason, "The Hawthorns, Framfield, near Uckfield, Sussex. Board and lodging, 12s. 6d. a week, and 5s. 3d. return ticket from London, available for a month. A stamped envelope should be enclosed to the secretary for her reply to any enquiries. We do not know whether any extension of time could be arranged for persons needing a longer rest.

A MEMBER writes to request that we will again bring the Scripture Reading and Prayer Union before our readers, so strongly recommended by the late Miss Frances Havergal. The organs of the Union are edited by the Rev. Ernest Boys, Beverley, Sidcup, Kent, one being the *Christian Progress Magazine*, and the other *Living Waters*. We have pleasure in complying with the request of our correspondent.

MARJORIE S.—One guinea a year is the tax charged for armorial bearings.

MARIE GORDON (India).—If the coloured picture should stick to the opposite page in the monthly numbers, it can very easily be set free by gently warming it before the fire.

WALTER KRUSE, of whose leaflet on "Bible Marking" to facilitate Bible study we gave a notice some time ago, writes to correct the address then given. His address is, Yew Tree Farm, Leeds, near Maidstone, Kent. It is not the Leeds in Yorkshire. We are glad his scheme has prospered.

DISCOURAGED.—The Married Women's Property Act would cover all your own possessions, both at the time of your marriage and afterwards. At the same time a careful inventory of furniture, etc., would be very desirable. A new Bill has been passed recently, which renders the position of a widow far better should her husband die intestate.

SOUTHSEA.—You had better arrange to go over to Boulogne by an early boat, and so leave yourself time to look for apartments before night. There is a line of steamers to Boulogne from London every day during the summer.

ROSEBUD.—It is a matter of taste and good feeling entirely as to whether you should wear your first wedding ring when you are married for the second time. The best test is, how you would like it if done to yourself were you in the other person's place. You should study your present husband's wishes.

PRINCESS had better apply to her father for protection, and tell him how she is treated. Her position is very hard, and we sympathise with her; but we feel sure all such trials of temper and patience are for our good, and will train us to be good "soldiers of Christ," "bearing hardness" for His sake, and showing love to those who persecute and treat us badly. But even so, "Princess" should ask her father's protection against personal violence.

POPPY.—Your "aunty" is right in requiring a little girl of eleven to wear pinafores. We advise you to add a "c" to the word denoting your dress. It should not be spelt "frok"; and the word "enough" is not written "inuff." But though "Poppy" should attend a little more to her spelling, her writing is good for her age.

BLACK ROOK.—1. Send to the washerwoman.—2. Poem very mediocre indeed!

KATHLEEN MAVOURNEEN should say, "My mother wishes you to do so and so," in giving orders for her mother to the servants.

LAURA.—It is the opinion of most writers on the subject that the tree that attains the greatest age, as a general rule, is the yew, that is to say, of all European trees. This distinction above its fellows of different genus may be realised as probably true when the history of the specimen at Brabourne, Kent, assigns to it, according to De Candolle, the prodigious age of 3,000 years! while one at Hedsor, Buckinghamshire, is said to be still more ancient. There is another at Fortingal, Perthshire, that is given 500 years less; and one in Derbyshire, to be seen in Darley Churchyard, 2,000. We may add to our list those of Fountains Abbey, Yorkshire, which are at the lowest computation 1,200 years old; and that at Ankerwyke House, Staines, is named as existing when Magna Charta was signed, in 1215, and as the place of rendezvous of Henry VIII. and Anne Boleyn. There is a grove of these remarkable trees at Norbury Park, Surrey, which dates back to the time of the Druids.

POOR POLLIE POLE.—There is a National Hospital for the Epileptic and Paralysed in Queen Square, Bloomsbury, W.C. Address the Secretary, Mr. B. Burford Rawlings. Also another hospital in Portland Terrace, Regent's Park (near St. John's Wood Road Station), where some patients are received free of charge, or on payment according to their means. Write to, or get some one to call on, Mr. H. Howgrave Graham, Secretary.

HYPERION.—Dew is produced by the condensation of watery vapour from the atmosphere by the cooling of the earth and vegetation bedewed. The radiation of their heat into open space produces this cooling as a natural consequence. As the sun sets and leaves them, they cool, though with unequal rapidity. Badly conducting solid matter does so rapidly, the atmosphere comparatively slowly; as do good conductors, if in contact with the earth, at a much slower rate, because the amount of warmth which they had lost they recover from the earth. The reason that the grass is so quickly covered with dew is the fact that it is the first to be deprived of the sunlight, is a bad conductor, and radiates well. Then the temperature at the level of the grass is some ten degrees colder than the air a few feet above it—say at an elevation of ten feet. Also, as stillness is essential to the formation of dew, the grass will be found quite wet when ever-moving branches and leaves of trees are comparatively dry. According to Dr. Dalton, the precipitation of dew annually in England is equal to five inches of rain.

VERA.—The hereditary successor of the sovereign (or the immediate heir) is his eldest son. The representative of H.R.H. the Prince of Wales is the Duke of Clarence and Avondale. And if the latter died without issue, his brother, Prince George of Wales, would be his successor.

M. CLARK (Austria).—Whatever may be the rank of those who may address you, you cannot err if you style them "Gnädige Frau." This applies to all German-speaking countries.

READER OF "G. O. P."—We do not recommend hair-washes excepting those home-made, such as rosemary tea, which is excellent, and may also be had from any chemist's shop. But you should refer to the articles by "Medicus" on the care of the hair.

many poems were presented to the Editor that in 1887 he remarked plaintively, "We wish our dear good girls would not send us such a quantity of verses to be criticised."

Two answers to would-be artists appearing next to each other in an 1885 issue present an interesting contrast:

MOLLY.—We cannot say much for the original sketches you enclose. We should think you had been reading a ghost book, or had been studying photographs of spirits, so spectral do they appear. One crazy girl appears about to throw herself over a precipice, and her companion, a thread paper creature, looks like the maiden all forlorn, but you omitted the cow with the crumpled horn.

NANNIE TORY.—Your drawings evince much talent. We should advise you to go to some school of art, and study thoroughly.

The answer to LADY NYASA in 1888 is still more encouraging, proving that readers were not invariably treated as, at best, harmless dilettantes:

The drawing you send is extremely well done; we should think you could make art a success, and regret to hear that you have to be taken from school. It is better for parents to practise economy in anything but this, as in the present day it is of the utmost importance to their children. We should suggest your going to the Birkbeck Institution, Chancery Lane, E.C., or to the Polytechnic, Regent Street, W., or to some school of art near you, and making every effort to keep up your studies, and in due season to pass those examinations you have not passed. In this way you will do much better for yourself and your parents, than by trying to find a situation when too young.

Two letters follow each other under the heading MUSIC in an issue of 1891:

PIANO, ORGAN, VIOLIN. The piece you send us bears all the marks of having been composed (as you say it was) in five minutes. Not quite up to our mark yet.

A MOTHER. We strongly advise you not to waste your time, nor your child's brain power, in obliging her to continue the laborious study of any mere accomplishment such as music, for which she has evidently no natural taste. Under such circumstances she could never make her attainments available for gaining a living; and your time and hers is too valuable to be wasted. Besides, she would prove a nuisance to all who heard her.

Questions about pets occur frequently. The Victorian dog appears to have had a thin time, unless it was an eccentric opinion of the Editor's that meat was bad for dogs, and that dog biscuits provided a healthier diet; and the Victorian parrot appears, judging by a number of queries, to have been given to the distressing habit of pulling out its own feathers. It is a relief to find that EDELWEISS is told:

Cats require warmth and kindness more almost than any creatures. They should never be turned out at night nor kept out of doors by day. [1885]

The girls do not confine themselves to queries about dogs, cats, parrots and canaries:

D.H. Your pet toad must be an idiot, or at least very deficient in natural instincts, if it cannot cater for itself; it knows better than you where to find its own food. [1886]

MUSIC.

VERENA.—In reply to your question "whether the semiquaver be played with the last quaver in the treble, or not, in playing a triplet of quavers with a quaver dot, and semiquaver in the bass?" you should play two quavers of the triplet with the dotted quaver, and the last quaver in the treble with the semiquaver in the bass. Perhaps the Prize Musical Improvement Society, which has a Harmony Correspondence Class, might suit you. The other clubs for musical improvement named in the "Dictionary of Girls' Clubs" are for practising only. Address, Miss Graham, 99, Bedford Street, Abercromby Square, Liverpool. The correspondence on harmony is 1s. a quarter, which, after all, is inexpensive, though so much more than mere practising clubs' fees.

OUR BESSIE should take the trouble of paying a visit to a music publisher and look through some of the exercises and pieces for the violin. We do not know what advance she has made in playing, nor whether, as yet, any at all. The people who serve in the shop will give her a choice suitable either for beginners or those more advanced.

LOVER OF MUSIC.—To be a professor of music you must go through a course of study in one of the colleges, and obtain certificates on passing certain examinations. There are several colleges in London; amongst them is the Guildhall School of Music. There are three terms of twelve weeks each, and the fees vary from £4 10s. to £11 1s. 6d. a term, according to the subjects taught, and the number of lessons given. There is also an entrance fee of 5s.

BASHFUL FIFTEEN.—There is no harm in your singing any more than the young birds attempting to do so, or the young cocks to crow, however hoarsely. What would be injurious is a regular course of training of the voice by a master, which should only begin, and very carefully too, when infancy is giving place to maturity. 2. You should hold the eye that is so blood-shot in an eye-glass full of very hot water when you go to bed, and avoid reading or doing fine work by candle or gaslight, and of exposing your eyes to a cold wind until quite recovered.

NINETEEN.—We cannot assist you in the matter of slowness in reading music. The acquirement of it rests with yourself. The strengthening of the fingers by rubbing with oil is recommended. Vaseline might still be better.

Above: answers to queries about music, January 25, 1890.

Far left: an interesting collection of replies, May 2, 1891.

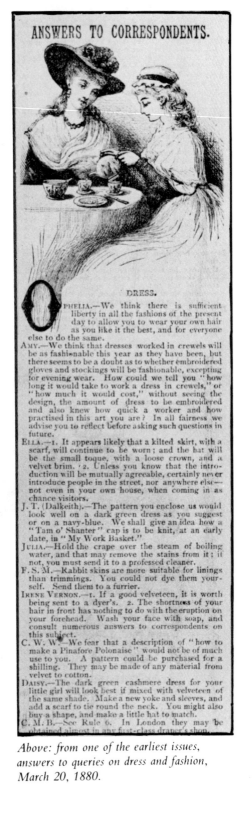

ANSWERS TO CORRESPONDENTS.

DRESS.

OPHELIA.—We think there is sufficient liberty in all the fashions of the present day to allow you to wear your own hair as you like it the best, and for everyone else to do the same.

AMY.—We think that dresses worked in crewels will be as fashionable this year as they have been, but there seems to be a doubt as to whether embroidered gloves and stockings will be fashionable, excepting for evening wear. How could we tell you "how long it would take to work a dress in crewels," or "how much it would cost," without seeing the design, the amount of dress to be embroidered and also knew how quick a worker and how practised in this art you are? In all fairness we advise you to reflect before asking such questions in future.

ELLA.—1. It appears likely that a kilted skirt, with a scarf, will continue to be worn; and the hat will be the small toque, with a loose crown, and a velvet brim. 2. Unless you know that the introduction will be mutually agreeable, certainly never introduce people in the street, nor anywhere else—not even in your own house, when coming in as chance visitors.

J. T. (Dalkeith).—The pattern you enclose us would look well on a dark green dress as you suggest or on a navy-blue. We shall give an idea how a "Tam o' Shanter" cap is to be knit, at an early date, in "My Work Basket."

JULIA.—Hold the crape over the steam of boiling water, and that may remove the stains from it; if not, you must send it to a professed cleaner.

F. S. M.—Rabbit skins are more suitable for linings than trimmings. You could not dye them yourself. Send them to a furrier.

IRENE VERNON.—1. If a good velveteen, it is worth being sent to a dyer's. 2. The shortness of your hair in front has nothing to do with the eruption on your forehead. Wash your face with soap, and consult numerous answers to correspondents on this subject.

C. W. W.—We fear that a description of "how to make a Pinafore Polonaise" would not be of much use to you. A pattern could be purchased for a shilling. They may be made of any material from velvet to cotton.

DAISY.—The dark green cashmere dress for your little girl will look best if mixed with velveteen of the same shade. Make a new yoke and sleeves, and add a scarf to tie round the neck. You might also buy a shape, and make a little hat to match.

C. M. B.—See Rule 6. In London they may be obtained almost in any first-class draper's shop.

Above: from one of the earliest issues, answers to queries on dress and fashion, March 20, 1880.

WENONA. Place your spider's nest under a small glass shade. [1885]

One wonders at the Editor's sangfroid in the latter case, unless the assumption was that the object was no longer inhabited.

A query which recurs frequently concerns a use for old postage stamps. The reply to AN ELDER SISTER in 1880 is:

No. Old postage stamps are of no use, except for the manufacture of "stamp snakes", which are very nice playthings for children. They require about 4,000 penny stamps for the body alone, while half-penny ones are needed for the tail. The head is made of black velvet, having bead eyes, but we think that you would require to see one, before you could manufacture one properly yourself.*

Etiquette is the subject of frequent enquiries:

CODLING.—The exclamation "Hang it!", although not swearing, is a vulgar slang expression. [1892]

IMPULSIVE.—If no one else were by to find his coat-sleeve for him, you were not guilty of any serious breach of etiquette in helping him to it. But such acts of friendship might lead to undesirable acquaintanceships, and you had better keep out of the way. You cannot safely perform such little attentions to strange men as a general rule. Were he a very old and infirm person it would be another matter. [1892]

TIBBIE.—If accompanied by your sisters (or one at least) you need feel no scruple in accepting the rector's Sunday hospitality, as you are helping his services by playing the organ. [1898]

A.B.C.—You were quite right in not returning the bow of any man with whom you were not acquainted. Girls who travel by train to school should be most particular in their conduct, and keep up an appearance of gravity and reserve. [1887]

HUGH, MAUD, AND GUS.—Never look at any strange man as you approach him in passing by, for sometimes a look may be taken advantage of by forward and impertinent men. Look straight onwards, and do not speak loud nor laugh in the street. It is generally a girl's own fault if she be spoken to, and, as such, is a disgrace to her, of which she should be ashamed to speak. But we must hope and believe that the liberties thus taken were owing to no light manner, nor indiscreet conduct in your case. [1881]

EUSTACIE wishes to know "up to what age a girl may climb a tree?" If a pack of wolves were after you, we should advise you to climb a tree up to ninety or a hundred! Otherwise, why make yourself look so like one of Dr Darwin's monkey-progenitors? [1880]

DUBBS.—It is not unladylike to ride a tricycle. It is enough to say that Her Majesty the Queen has patronised it for her granddaughters. But your dress may be unsuitable for it, and you may hold yourself ungracefully, and work the pedals in an ungainly way. If your elbows be spread out, your head much bent forward, and your dress be so ill-arranged as to show your stockings to a considerable extent, the general appearance behind will be decidedly inelegant and froglike. [1885]

---

* A "stamp snake" appears in the illustration on page 36.

SACK.—How comes it that you sometimes walk with a gentleman, if not engaged to him? If your intended husband, you may, of course, walk under one umbrella; but otherwise you had better keep your own to yourself. If needing one, he can buy one as well as you can. [1885]

BLACK AND WHITE.—It would be utterly unseemly, and as much as your reputation is worth, to walk out at night with any man but your father or brother. There are certain rules of society, in the lower and middle classes as well as in the higher, which were made by common consent, for the protection of young women, and this is one—that they should not be out in the streets or roads at night, unless under the care of a member of the family or middle-aged woman. You should get home before dark, if possible; and always be accompanied by a friend, if walking (even by daylight), with a man to whom you are not engaged. [1892]

PANSY.—Why uncertain in a question of thanking for any little attention paid you? Be sure of one thing, that you can never err on the side of graciousness, and no trifling act on the part of another is too insignificant to be accepted with a kindly acknowledgment. Always say "I am obliged to you for your escort", or words to that effect. [1901]

Perhaps my favourite reply on the subject of etiquette is the following, addressed to PERPLEXITY in 1891:

We can see no cause for perplexity in such a case as yours. The man who sent you a mouse in a match-box could scarcely be called a "gentleman", and such vulgar practical jokes are unknown in "polite society".

The *G.O.P.* could not invariably provide what was asked for. EMILY FRANCES must have been disappointed to be told in 1886, "We cannot undertake to give a recipe for making woollen parrots." Perhaps understandably, the query put by HURLY-BURLY in 1880 received in reply only another question: "Are you serious in asking 'whether eating eggs, and wearing high-heeled shoes, make you deaf'?"

Some of the replies are mysterious, such as this to ELLEN in 1886: "They are, and always will be so, although not universally worn, nor ever will be." (Beards? Hats? Corsets?) The following at first glance seems even more baffling:

E.E.E. (Cape Colony).—We know all about the appliance to which you refer, and strongly advise you never to use it again. It is, as it were, a stepping-stone to what is highly dangerous and evil; and many who have made a toy of it have discovered its real character, and destroyed it. [1889]

A flash of inspiration—could the nasty thing have been an ouija board? Present-day magazine correspondents tend to be uninspired in their choice of pseudonym, all too frequently settling for WORRIED. Those of the Victorian *Girl's Own Paper* are of a far richer variety, verging, indeed, on the rococo. Among them are TEAPOT, COREOPSIS TINCTORIA, THE TOAD, A PRINCESS OF THULE, THE DAUGHTER OF AN IRISH LANDLORD, MAD CRICKETER, MARQUIS POFFWHISKER, A BASHFUL YOUNG POTATO, QUEEN OF THE WUNKS and DISTRESSED CRUMPET. After these, a mere PERPLEXED tends to pale.

Serious family problems are dealt with from time to time. Questions about marital difficulties are not frequent, but V.I.S. is advised in 1887,

WORK.

JANIE.—Finding that you and one or two other readers have not been able to work the "Fly pattern tricot stripe," described on page 332 of our March number, we gladly re-write it, making some slight alterations, by which means we hope all difficulty will be removed. Commence by making a chain of twelve stitches. 1st Row.—Miss two, tricot one to end of row, you will then have five loops on the needle; make four chain into the last loop in chain. 2nd Row.—Take off first loop on needle, make one chain, take off *two* together, continue making one and taking off two to end of row. 3rd Row.—Make three chain, * draw a loop through the first open space, a second through the perpendicular stitch, and a third through the second opening, take off *three* together, make one chain, and repeat from *, commencing in the same space as last worked into. Make four chain in the third chain stitch at the end of row. These *two* last rows are to be worked until the stripe is the length required. The number and colour of the stripes must depend upon the size and purpose for which the couvrette is intended.

Above: queries about work (in the sense of handicrafts) were often sent in (June 18, 1881).

"Your sister could certainly get a separation, and could protect herself and property from her worthless husband, and she could punish him if he were caught." And MAUD in 1886:

Go to the police office and inform the inspector of your trouble and the cruel treatment to which you are subjected, and he will take you to the proper quarters, where you may obtain a separation and an allowance. Do nothing rashly and nothing wrong, be your trials and provocations what they may. What you suggested to us would be very wrong indeed, and we think and hope you must have done so under great excitement. If by word or act you thoughtlessly gave cause for jealousy, you might not obtain the separation and allowance, to which otherwise you could lay just claim. Pray God to guide you and preserve you from evil.

LIZZIE HASLAM is told in 1883:

Your little nephew and niece—who are dependent on your support, as well as motherly care (being orphans), and who at so tender an age refuse to obey you or to call you "auntie", as in their mother's lifetime—should be punished until you can again bring them under control. Try mild measures, such as standing them in a corner, or take away their toys for a time; this failing, give a good slap or two with your own hand on theirs, and if the rebellion be too determined for this to put it down, nothing remains then to be done but to give the unruly little people a good sound whipping. Instant obedience must be obtained, or later on your authority will be irretrievably gone, and they will grow up without due moral training.

What story can have lain behind A.C.'s letter to elicit this reply in 1889:

Could you not arrange with your clergyman or minister to come and have an interview with the wild, unmanageable girl—unexpectedly to her—and let him tell her of the injury to her character and her future prospects in life this conduct of hers must be. You could not send her to a reformatory, unless she were guilty of some criminal offence. If the clergyman's representations have no effect in shaming her, you had better consult him as to any school at which she could be placed, or she might perhaps be sent to some quiet distant place—put to service in a farmhouse, where there would be a strict hand over her.

The sense of family duty was strong throughout the epoch. The great majority of marriages were made for life, but the risk of early death meant that a widowed parent might be left with a number of small children to care for, or faced with years of loneliness. In an early issue (November, 1880), a reply from the Editor deals firmly with the question of a parent's remarriage:

PERPLEXITY.—You are very cruel and quite in the wrong to annoy your father about his second marriage. As there seems to be nothing against the new wife, you have no right to resent the union and to talk about leaving home. We know a case of a dying wife making her husband promise never to re-marry, and the man's life was a wretched and lonely one ever afterwards. We also know of girls who love, and justly so, their stepmothers very dearly and do not consider it an injustice to the memory of their own mother. Your writing is rather nice.

Proper family feeling is set out still more plainly when the Editor answers a later enquiry from bereaved daughters, and one from a restless teenager:

Far right: a page of answers to correspondents in the style of the later issues (March 9, 1901).

162

ANSWERS TO CORRESPONDENTS.

STUDY AND STUDIO.

MISS BIRRELL, 31, Lansdowne Crescent, Glasgow, sends us a prospectus of the Queen Margaret Correspondence Classes, for S. I. We regret that our rules forbid us to forward matter by post in connection with this column, but we cordially recommend the classes to our readers. They prepare for examinations of various grades, and also assist students in private studies. The Hon Sec., Miss Birrell, will be glad to give all information.

WANDA DE GORKIEWICZ.—Many thanks for your delightful letter, which interested us very greatly. We are glad you have received so many cards, and are informing our correspondents that you are no longer at the High School, Constantinople.

MISS HENRIETTA M. CROSFIELD, noticing our answer to PANSY, suggests *Easy Lessons in Egyptian Hieroglyphics*, by E. A. Wallis Budge, published by Kegan Paul at 3s. 6d. *First Steps in Egyptian*, by the same author, costs 12s. We thank MISS CROSFIELD for her kind letter.

MISS F. O. ANDERSON, Lea Hall, Gainsboro', Lincolnshire, asks us to mention her Literary Club for amateurs, in which prose compositions are criticised and circulated bi-monthly. All particulars as to rules, etc., will be forwarded on application.

ONE OF PEGGY'S FRIENDS.—We should paraphrase the lines by Burns something as follows:—When life is bright and all goes merrily, it is comparatively easy to stifle the conscience and to disregard religion in pleasure; but let dark days come, and the mind be troubled and tempest-tossed, then will be felt the need of "the anchor for the soul" which is given by Christianity.

*** We have pleasure in directing our readers' attention to competitions at the Royal Academy of Music for the Goring Thomas and the Dove Scholarships. The Goring Thomas Scholarship offers free tuition for three years at the Royal Academy. It will be awarded to that British-born candidate of either sex who may show the greatest promise of ability as composer of lyrical dramatic works. The Dove Scholarship is of the value of about £32 yearly for three years. It will be awarded to that candidate of either sex who may show such talent in violin-playing as to give promise of future distinction. The literary examination for each competition will be held on Monday, April 29th, 1901, and the Musical Competition on Wednesday, May 1st, 1901. Full particulars may be obtained from the Secretary, Royal Academy of Music, Tenterden Street, Hanover Square, London, W.

INTERNATIONAL CORRESPONDENCE.

Exchange of view post-cards is requested by (MISS) NELLIE H. RAE, Raeburn, Hamilton, Scotland; SOPHIE GARBEA, Horezani, Gara Bibesci, Jud Gorjiu, Roumania; ELSIE BIGGS, Station Road, Victoria, Australia (Australasian stamps or a card for foreign stamps or a card); MAY GRAHAM, Station Road, Otahuhu, Auckland, New Zealand; MILICENT McCLATCHIE, 62, Edith Road, West Kensington, London, W.; S. TACHDJIAN, 115, Grande Rue de Pera, Constantinople (views of Constantinople offered for all others, except those of England and France); MARGARET SPEEDIE, Surrey Road, South Yarra, Melbourne, Victoria, Australia; LILY TROLLIP, Spring Valley, Bushman's Kop, Orange River Colony, S. Africa (cards for postage stamps, especially Mexican, not less than eight).

MISS E. M. DALE, Post Chalmers, New Zealand, writes to inform MISS L. HARDENBROEK that she has sent post-cards and New Zealand stamps to the address first given.

ELSIE G. JONES, 27, Southfield Road, Middlesboro', Yorkshire, would like a girl about 14, in England or abroad, to write to her.

MISCELLANEOUS.

MERCIER.—We have given articles on the subject—illustrated ones—in this magazine within the last two or three months. Look back yourself and you will find them. These may suffice without purchasing a book on calisthenics.

J. W. G.—Are you acquainted with the "Governesses' Benevolent Institution"? It gives temporary assistance to those in distress, has an annuity fund, a provident fund, an asylum for the aged, etc. Secretary, C. W. Klugh, Esq., 32, Sackville Street, W. There is a "Governesses' Guild," 139, Fulham Road, S.W. The former would, we think, meet your requirements.

CHERRY and MOTHER'S HELP.—With reference to making the eyelashes grow see our answer to "Lord Roberts." As to making your nose "thinner by pinching the end of it," we do not think it would, but it might inflame and make it red. We do not approve of any attempt to thin yourself unless a doctor pronounced you to have "fatty degeneration of the heart," in which case he would prescribe for you and watch your case. Taking much butter, cream, and fatty foods might be limited to a certain degree, however, without injury to the system in general.

A QUAVER.—The Royal College of Organists, Hart Street, Bloomsbury, W.C., admits women, by examination on equal terms with men, to fellowship and associateship; and should you be desirous of making way as an organist, you should pass their examinations, which are held half-yearly, and consist of solo-playing tests and paper work. There are not many openings for women, however, except in small country churches, we are told.

BLACK EYES, ETC.—Hardy ferns do well in a north aspect, and so do the following plants: myosotis, mimulus, violas, pansies, vincas or periwinkles, and hardy primulas, the lily of the valley, hydrangeas, ivies, and clematis, and some climbing roses, such as the Dundee Rambler.

CLAUDIA.—We have answered your question many times. Those who fail to understand our Lord's words recorded by St. Matthew (xii. 31, 32) and St. Mark (iii. 28, 29) have overlooked the explanation given in the 30th verse of the last-named chapter, i.e., "Because they said, He hath an unclean spirit"; and in verse 22, "He hath Beelzebub, and by the prince of the devils casteth He out devils." Now, reflect a moment. If our Blessed Lord was possessed by Satan and his evil spirits, He could not be the incarnate, only-begotten Son of God, and in this case there could not have been any atonement for man, and His sacrifice on the Cross was of no avail for our salvation. So those who reject Him as their divine Redeemer cannot be saved through Him; and in regarding Him as doing all things through the power of the devil, they necessarily reject Him as their saviour. They place themselves outside the pale of salvation, and so long as they reject him as the pure and holy One, the God-Man, One with the Father and the Holy Ghost, and deny that His miracles were performed by the indwelling omnipotent power of the Holy Ghost, they simply cut themselves off from participation in the redemption wrought by Him. They are living in a reprobate state; they blaspheme the divinity that dwelt and acted in Him. How could one possessed by devils and unclean spirits be a Saviour to them?

LORD ROBERTS.—We are not sure that your eyelashes would grow again if you cut them. Were they in the habit of growing, they would be hanging down over your cheeks by this time.

M. A. S.—Photographers will tell you that to take the shiny sort of glaze off a photograph before painting it they pass the tongue over the surface. This is one of the little secrets of the art.

Above: miscellaneous replies of August 21, 1880. This particular issue included predictable advice to STEPHANOTIS, *grieving over a disappointment—"Try to do something useful for others"—and referred* VIOLET *to her doctor with the austere comment, "It is not seemly to describe your ailments on a postcard."*

BIRTHDAY.—It seems very strange for loving daughters to inquire, "What month would it be etiquette for us to go to a dance, our dear mother having died very early in February?" Seven months only had elapsed (when writing in September) since that "dear mother" was laid in her grave; and you are eager to go to a dance in the first month that mere "etiquette" would permit. What has "etiquette" to do with the love and respect you should feel for your mother, and the sense of an irreparable loss? You ought to wear the deepest mourning for a year; and how soon, after that, you would like to go to that kind of entertainment, it is for you to decide. How would your father like it? Would he consider it both loving and respectful? [1894]

F.C.J.—Every girl should be so educated as to be able to support herself if necessary. So long, however, as the necessity for your leaving home does not exist, it is your duty to endeavour to remain there, to be a comfort, as a daughter might be in a thousand little ways, to her parents. They have had the expense of your education, and of all else you have enjoyed, and to arrange to leave them the moment your schooling is over, and to make no return in those watchful loving attentions that mere gratitude demands of you, not to speak of filial affection, would be a most discreditable and undutiful act. How could you be "dull at home?" You might be engaged in perfecting your education in so many ways—in housekeeping, cookery, nursing, reading, and plain needlework. The proper place for a little girl in her "teens" is at home, when not at school. We feel sure that it was only want of due reflection—not want of natural affection, or, at least, good feeling—that made you contemplate a removal from home when your schooling shall be over. We request the attention of all our girl readers to this answer. [1884]

AN ORPHAN GIRL (1882) writes in some anxiety about the brother for whom, it seems, she keeps house, and is told:

Merely talking to your brother will not suffice to keep him at home at night if he be a pleasure-seeker. Perhaps if you could invite some pleasant and suitable companions to the house to tea, from time to time; had music, and practised glee or chorus singing; or introduced some small games, and made home bright and cheerful, he might find it more agreeable than his haunts outside. Do not grumble and look doleful, but let him see that you try to make home more attractive.

Many of the correspondents ask if the Editor can suggest ways of earning money at home. Sadly, there is little he can advise:

DOG ROSE.—Perhaps in your position as an only daughter, with an invalid mother, you may do more by saving than by earning. Make yourself a good housekeeper, dressmaker and general needlewoman, and you will soon make a great many shillings by your helpful ways. [1880]

However, readers regularly ask for and receive information and guidance on careers. Here the answers are almost invariably careful and informed:

A. R. LEWIS.—Naturally, the constant use of the telephone is injurious, creating what M. Gellé calls "aural over-pressure". The working of the telegraphic apparatus, and constant attendance amidst the jar and noise of machinery, likewise tend to overstrain the ear and to induce nervous excitability, giddiness, and neuralgic pains. But how long the delicate nerves may be exposed to this over-pressure without inducing any of these evil results we are unable to tell you. Only it is well, when choosing a vocation in life, to look beyond the present into such possible eventualities; and if of a nervous temperament, and at all subject to headache and neuralgic pains, it would be well to choose some other calling. [1896]

TRIXY.—The salaries earned by librarians of either sex are so low that we are not inclined to recommend you to think of such work. At the same time, if you are really drawn to it by fondness for books, there would be no harm in writing to the head librarians of the public libraries in the towns you mention, and asking them whether they could receive a woman assistant. In the Manchester Free Libraries women are considerably employed as assistants at very small salaries. At the People's Palace, London, women enjoy better positions, but there are few of them. [1897]

JESSIE A. PINKER.—At the London National Training School for Cookery, Buckingham Palace Road, S.W., the training for the post of Cookery Instructor in all branches of plain cooking costs 13 guineas for the full course of twenty-four weeks. You will find further particulars as to cookery instruction in London in our articles *What is the London County Council doing for Girls?* (March). But we have made further enquiries and it seems highly probable that you will be able to obtain what you want at the new Municipal Technical School, Brighton.... As the building is not yet completed ... perhaps your daughter could stay a little longer at school till the classes ... are fully established. We are gratified to learn that, having taken the *Girl's Own Paper* as a girl, you now take it for your own girls, and consider its influence "like that of a sweet and gentle lady". [1897]

Sometimes a warning note is sounded:

LILLIE MORE.—We feel very much the enormous responsibility that you have placed upon us in asking us to advise you on entering the profession to which you refer. But we dare not do other than counsel you to abandon all ideas of thus engaging yourself. Believe us you are not alone in your particular aspirations. Most girls above the ordinary abilities have the same unhealthy craving at some particular period of their life, but when they grow older and see how incongruous is that position to a good honest girl's they are filled with a life-long thankfulness that they did not join the profession. In addition to great abilities, unusual physical strength, and personal attractions, a Christian girl or woman would need the steadfastness of a more than Job or St Paul to come out unscathed from the fiery ordeal. We happen to know many things of the life and character of the lady you mention which would lead you to either despise or pity her very much. [1880]

Did LILLIE hope to follow Mrs Langtry as an artist's model—or to go on the stage?

Questions about religion are not uncommon in these pages, and the answers are generally long and serious:

KITTY SCOTT and LAURA.—Judging from the questions perpetually asked, our young converts seem to regard conversion as consisting in denying themselves certain amusements (music, etc.), various articles of women's usual dress, and restriction in reading religious books. Religion is not of a negative, but positive and active, character. [1884]

OLIVE.—You say you are "greatly troubled" about the thoughts with which you are beset. Now, so long as you are "troubled", you have the evidence in yourself that God has *not* "given you up to hardness of heart." Do you not remember what St Paul says in his Epistle to the Romans vii., 20, "now, if I do that I would not, it is no more I that do it, but sin that dwelleth in me." Sin confessed, repudiated, prayed against, and fought against, is sin forgiven, and atoned for by the bloodshedding of Christ....
Your letter is very well expressed. [1883]

appreciation on "Marion's" part. It is so nicely written too! Kind hearted-Heppie.

FLORENCE.—Choose the handwriting you most admire, and copy it carefully. We once knew a girl who quite changed hers in six weeks by so doing.

HAPPY DOT.—James Montgomery is the author of a poem called "A Mother's Love."

ZARA.—A turkey carpet looks best when frequently shaken.

A. G. B.—We could not recommend you to take a situation on the Continent, unless you know exactly to whom you are going. The English chaplain in Paris, in a recent number of the *Times*, begs English girls to stay at home, and details the miseries of many who have gone there to be swindled, and left penniless and friendless.

CLARA and ANON.—Brush the leather which has been inked with a solution of oxalic acid in water. Your second query is not one we should answer. Read "How to Look My Best."

IVY and MAY.—There is no way of pressing leaves or flowers except between leaves of blotting-paper, or else by ironing with a warm iron.

TAMMY.—Are you quite serious when you ask us to "explain the working" of a "scent fountain" which we have never seen? Write to the manufacturer.

LILY OF THE VALLEY.—The words are those of a very ordinary ballad song, apparently. You might inquire of a music seller.

TWO RING DOVES.—Doves are grain eaters. Give them peas, barley, wheat, and tares, a little hemp-seed, small beans, a little rock-salt to peck at, crumbs of bread, and plenty of gravel and water.

FLOSSY.—1. See answer to "Ivy and May." The voice is trained by practice. 2. Very hard brushes are not good for the hair. You have spelt envelope rightly.

JESSIE.—1. We know of no other method for curing a habit of stooping than wearing a face-board stuck into a belt in front for a certain time daily while reading or working, and a fixed resolution to remember and check the habit all the rest of the day. 2. It is impossible to lay down a rule that will apply to all alike in reference to suppers. Much depends on the hour of the previous meal, and that of retiring to bed, on the nature of the supper, and on the state of health, and on the individual peculiarities of the person who hesitates about eating just before bed-time. A heavy meal at a late hour could not be wholesome for any one, for the body is fatigued, and the digestive powers are thereby enfeebled. Some sleep the better for partaking of a slight refreshment, others do not. Those who sleep little, and have some hours of fasting before them, would probably be benefited by taking a biscuit and a small cup of broth; or of milk with a teaspoonful of lime-water in it.

Above: some other miscellaneous replies to readers' letters, June, 1880.

THREE ENGLISH GIRLS, GERMANY, sent in a query on extra-terrestrial life in 1884. They are told:

We consider it to be utterly absurd to imagine that our little world should be the only speck in the vast universe of worlds—either within or beyond our view—that is inhabited by intelligent beings, and acquainted with their Almighty Creator. But how many may be fallen like ourselves and needing a Saviour, has not of course been revealed to us. The side of our own little satellite the moon, which is turned towards us, presents the appearance of a world destroyed by volcanic action. Many may be so. But even this would not necessarily preclude its being inhabited by disembodied spirits, or bodies having different attributes and constitutions to ours. All is veiled in mystery for the present.

The usual practice of the *G.O.P.* was to print answers only, but on occasion readers' letters did appear. In June, 1883, an issue includes *A Dip into the Editor's Correspondence*. Nine letters are printed, among them one from A HAPPY YOUNG WIFE:

DEAR MR EDITOR.—Pray forgive me for troubling you, but as I have taken your most charming paper from the first, and have only written to you once, I think you will not be very cross at my writing to thank you for a good husband and a comfortable home. I wish you could come and stay with us, we would try to make you enjoy your visit.

No doubt you wonder how you can possibly have aided such a happy state of affairs: it just happened like this. When *The Girl's Own Paper* first appeared three years ago I was twenty-five, and never had received an offer of marriage. As I had always been taught to consider that woman's first duty was to marry, you may suppose I was in rather a melancholy, discontented state of mind, but thanks to my dear *Girl's Own Paper*, both from tales and articles, and most of all from the "Answers to Correspondents", I learnt differently, and tried by God's blessing to fill my life with work for Him. I took up French, music, etc., which I had sadly neglected, asked for and got a district, and determined by God's help if I were to be an old maid I would at least be a contented one and make others happy....

I had quite left off thinking of the possibility of marriage for myself, when I was electrified by receiving a proposal from a gentleman much my superior. He tells me how that he was first attracted to me by the bright, contented expression of my face and total lack of self-consciousness. So you see, dear Mr Editor, I have indeed great cause to be truly grateful to *The Girl's Own Paper*....

In this batch of nine letters are three of praise and gratitude from Australia, one from Hungary, and one from Italy.

The volume of overseas readers swelled increasingly as the years went by, until in January, 1901, the Editor started a new column, *International Correspondence*, in which readers sought correspondents in foreign countries:

E. N. DRUMMOND ... Dublin, asks for a French girl correspondent aged 16 or 17, each to write in her own language, and inquires whether Miss Natalie Gorianoff of St Petersburg would care for an Irish correspondent.

Very often an exchange of more than mere letters is proposed:

MISS DAISY and MISS EDITH LE FONTAINE ... Smyrna, Asia Minor, would like to correspond and exchange stamps with girls in Italy, Spain, Norway, Hungary and America. The former will send Turkish, Levant, and Persian stamps to anybody who will send her a few humming-birds' eggs.

Below: a page of answers adorned with two line decorations which admirably sum up the G.O.P.'s unfailing advice to readers (March, 1881).

I.—BEFORE SUBSCRIBING TO "THE GIRL'S OWN PAPER."

WORK.

MARCH.—Read "Seasonable Dress," and have your dresses made very wide in the chest, and endeavour to correct your round shoulders by constant care and thought. Black silk should be chosen with a moderate sized rib, a very large one generally denotes the presence of cotton. Purchase at a good shop where they care for their reputation. Your writing is very neat and clean.

IRISH BIDDIE.—We should send the black silk velvet to a cleaner's. A recipe for reviving black cloth is given at page 316, vol i.

MITTEN THUMB.—To knit the thumb on a mitten see page 144, vol. i.

FLO.—We regret we cannot assist you to dispose of your mother's work. Try a draper's or a fancy wool shop.

AGNES.—Make a narrow hem for the top of your frilling, not a roll. The whipping is very well performed.

MADCAP.—Trim the pale violet dress with deep red satin or silk broché. Select the right shade carefully.

ART.

MARGUERITE.—The outline of flowers for painting should be carefully drawn in pencil, not too hard nor black, as as to prevent their subsequent erasure. Your writing is very legible and neat, and your note well expressed and ladylike.

LITTLE BUTTERCUP.—Varnish the whole plate if you do not admire the white look of it. It will keep much cleaner also.

BARBARA.—Spirits of wine and turpentine are used to clean pictures and to dissolve the hard old varnish; but they will attack the paint as well if not washed off at the proper time with cold water. Your varnish must have been poor or badly mixed.

COOKERY.

EDITH CHURCH.—We are quite at a loss to understand your difficulty, as nothing can be more explicit than the directions given on page 28. "Rinsed out of boiling water, squeezed dry, and floured well," is surely simple enough? Your writing might be improved by writing copies.

A YOUNG COOK.—1. We cannot give addresses nor recommend "kitcheners." 2. Inquire at a music-seller's.

THE DAISY CHAIN.—For toffee recipes, see pages 15 and 176, vol. i. You should be guided by your schoolmistress.

MISCELLANEOUS.

LOCH LEVEN.—The name of the Navigators' Islands was given to them by their discoverer, from his observing the natives to be in possession of superior canoes, which they managed with the most dexterous skill. Your writing should be more flowing and free.

MURIEL.—There is no occasion for bowing to a gentleman whom you do not know. Your writing is not pretty though so legible.

J. O. U. W.—1. "Primrose way" appears another way of saying "flowery way," or "gay spring-like paths." Shakespeare used the same expression in *Hamlet*, act i., scene 3. And a recent author, Motley, also makes use of it in the same poetical way. 2. It is better to take your parents' advice as to your reading.

C. P. C.—"Ling's Exercises," which have been translated by Dr. Roth, would perhaps suit you.

ENILEC.—We should advise you to have your hand well rubbed with fresh lard, which will probably give strength and lessen the stiffness. Thank you for your kind letter.

SWEETBRIAR.—The 4th March, 1863, was Wednesday. Your writing is anything but good for your age, and you would do well to take to copies again.

DISRAELINA.—We think you have mistaken the initials. Your writing is very good.

AN ONLY CHILD.—See page 624, vol. i., on the falling of hair, also 80 and 111; also the articles at pages 259, 400, and 416. We thank you for your kind letter.

MADELINE MURPHY.—Ammonia might affect the colour of some things perhaps, you had better make a trial before using it.

VIC.—Perhaps your garden soil is not suitable for fern culture, or you do not give them moisture enough.

MARY CARPENTER.—1. Thank you for your suggestion. We think our paper is sufficiently general to be useful to every class of life. 2. We hear that there is a very clever new seat for using behind the counter just patented, and now that a practical step forward has been taken like this, we hope the "standing evil" may be overcome. Thank you very much for your kind expressions of satisfaction with our efforts.

FIDUS ACHATES.—The gentleman's mother would pay the first visit. Fish is eaten with a fish knife and fork. If these are absent, with a fork.

MIDSHIPMAN EASY.—It would be impossible to say, we think, who first invented rudders. The first people who tried navigation probably.

POPPY.—Read "Sketching from Nature," page 23, vol. ii.

POLLIE FLINDERS.—Your writing is not good for your age.

COLLEEN BAWN.—Thank you for your kind letter.

SNOWDROP.—See article on "Puddings," at page 27, vol. ii. Your writing is clear and legible.

AN INQUIRER.—Gently and kindly tell your friend that it is a duty to refrain from "playing with edged tools"; and that no greater evidences of a pure and straightforward friendship in private than can be honestly manifested in public. A religious person will not only abstain from evil known and undisputed, but from all that is even doubtfully permissible. The more your friend trusts you the more scrupulous you should be.

CARROTS.—You do not say of what substance the white tracings on the black marble are composed. Perhaps the groove might be filled in with white paint. Should you see a similar style of decoration in any clock shop, inquire of the manufacturers.

A CONSTANT SUBSCRIBER.—Table-cloths are used at afternoon tea, and at a late tea substituting a late dinner. A long napkin or cloth should be laid over the sideboard, but not to hang down at the front. You write fairly well.

TEASE OF STRETFORD.—A little girl of sixteen writes to inquire whether, at that time of life, she should be "cold and proud," and whether she should "ponder and screw." We fail to understand what she does when she performs the operation called "screwing." We have heard of "screwing-in a waist," and hope she does not contemplate any practice so baneful and silly. Let her be gentle, modest, and natural, putting on no "airs" of any kind. When well in health and kindly cared for, and trying to do her little duties well, she could not be other than "lively and gay," instead of, as "T. S." expresses it, "cold and proud." 2. "Navy blue" would suit our little correspondent very well.

CISSY writes, "Will you kindly take pity on me, for I am a very poor girl?" We would willingly express our sympathy, for we love all our readers, and especially those who are in trouble. But surely, Cissy should tell us the cause of her unhappiness. Cissy is asked to furnish us with particulars that we might know how to help her.

J. H.—Your verses have the merit of earnestness, but are not up to the standard required for publication.

CORA ORMAN.—1. Read "Health and Beauty for the Hair," which appeared in vol. i. 2. A verse of some good Easter hymn would be suitable for the memorial card. Such a verse, for instance, as :—

"Lord, by the stripes which wounded Thee
  From death's dread sting Thy servants free,
  That we may live and sing to Thee
                                  Alleluia!"

Your writing needs improvement ; there is no character in it.

DAMASK ROSE.—We have received a long illegible letter from you, which we *think* is sent to inform us that we have not answered previous letters sent by you. We suppose that they were equally badly written, and so received the fate of being instantly destroyed, or that we had others worthier of the space.

II.—AFTERWARDS.

1819

1901

[Price One Penny.

Above: the memorial notice published in the issue of February 16, following Queen Victoria's death on January 22, 1901.

Whether he liked it or not, the Editor seems by 1901 to be acting as a Post Office:

We have a letter for KOMURASKI SAN, with a silver leaf from Table Mountain and some African stamps.

168

ART STUDENTS AT BREAKFAST IN PARIS.

Trustfully, readers continued to write from all over the world, seeking the Editor's advice which, blunt or not, was always straightforward. One reply, to a letter from CUSHILDA D.C. in 1888, may be said to embody the philosophy of *The Girl's Own Paper* in its first twenty-one years, although that philosophy was often expressed less sternly:

Your chief desire in leaving school early is to go the sooner to balls and parties every night. Alas! What a frivolous idea! Is this the object of existence? Have you no work in life to accomplish? Have you, to say the least, no idea of the duties of home life in "requiting your parents", devoting your mind, strength, and all you have learnt at school (paid for by them) to do them loving service and add to the comfort and cheerfulness of home? What are you going to do with the talents committed to you by your Divine Master—health, time, education, competent means, and knowledge of the way of holiness and salvation? A little schoolgirl of fifteen has three more years of school discipline, and then, at the very least, three more of home-work and education, literary and practical. "Knowing a lot of German and drawing well", you might only be a poor little empty-headed nonentity.

Above: the last illustration from the last issue of 1901, the year which marked the opening of the Edwardian era and the magazine's "coming of age" at twenty-one. Very different from the girls in the line illustrations of twenty years earlier, these students, photographed in Paris, are enjoying a picnic breakfast in public, and three of them are even bare-headed.

"THREE LITTLE MAIDS FROM SCHOOL."

A HAPPY ENDING.

The Editor, Charles Peters, and his staff were professional journalists. They had to sell their magazine, and to do that they had to give the readers what they wanted in exchange for their pennies. Yet, looking through these old Annuals, one feels the desire of the writers not only to entertain, nor even only to inform and instruct, but to guide, influence and mould. The readers were "our girls"; the writers wrote, in general, as adults to girls, or sometimes as adults to slightly younger adults, not as teenagers to teenagers. Obviously they aimed at satisfying their readers, and if they had not succeeded in doing so, the magazine would never have seen the new century; but perhaps they did much more than that.

However that may be, the *Girl's Own Paper* must have played its part in making the Victorian girl and the Edwardian woman what she was. The magazines of the late twentieth century are, in their turn, playing their part towards shaping the women of the twenty-first. Journalists do well to remember it.

Above: the closing instalment of The Studio Mariano *by Eglanton Thorne (April 2, 1892).*

Far left: three schoolgirls dressed for the autumn term, from How a Girl Should Dress, *by "Norma": August 31, 1901.*

INDEX

Page references to illustrations are given in italic type. Captions (*cap.*) are indexed only if they do not appear on the same page as the illustrations to which they refer.

Chapter headings are given in small caps.

Titles are indexed in *italic* type. The genre "fiction" includes short stories, serials, and story features. The genre "article" includes series of articles as well as one-off items and features.

British royalties are indexed by their Christian name, members of the peerage by their title.

Pseudonyms are given in inverted commas.

If a reference runs over two or more pages (*e.g.* 112–118), those pages may include illustration material which does not bear directly on the item being indexed.

"DON'T LOOK SO SAD, MY DEAR, ANOTHER VOLUME IS ABOUT TO COMMENCE."